The Edge of the Wilderness

Portrait of the artist; 1903.

The Edge of the Wilderness

A Portrait of the Canadian North

Frank E. Schoonover

Edited by
Cortlandt Schoonover

Methuen

Toronto London
Sydney Wellington

Library of Congress Catalogue Card
Number 74-83843
ISBN 0-458-91080-5

Printed and bound in Canada
by the Bryant Press Limited, Toronto.

78 77 76 75 74   1 2 3 4 5 6

Contents

Acknowledgments

Dr. Jules Noel Wright, University of Guelph, Ontario, whose broad appreciation of the talented devotion of Frank E. Schoonover to a lifelong portrayal of the Canadian North Country inspired the production of this book, and who assisted greatly in its writing.

Mr. John Randall Schoonover, grandson of Frank E. Schoonover, and owner and conservator of his studio in Wilmington, Delaware, whose unflagging assistance in the details of material assembly and knowledgeable additions and interpretations deserve utmost appreciation.

The editor's wife, Naomi, whose original concept of this book and whose patient and professional devotion to all phases of its completion make her the one most enthusiastically responsible for it.

For invaluable assistance and cooperation: The Glenbow-Alberta Institute, Calgary, Alberta, Canada; The Brandywine Art Museum, Chadd's Ford, Pennsylvania; The Delaware Art Museum, Wilmington, Delaware; The University of Delaware, Newark, Delaware.

Sincere thanks is given to the following publishers for permission to reprint stories by Frank E. Schoonover: Charles Scribner's Sons, Harper's Magazine, Incorporated, Sprague Publishing Company.

Grateful acknowledgement to all owners of paintings and photographs is made under each item reproduced. By special request of some owners, however, their names have been withheld.

Frank Herzog, whose skill in photographing the original works of Frank E. Schoonover has been an invaluable contribution to the book.

Cortlandt Schoonover

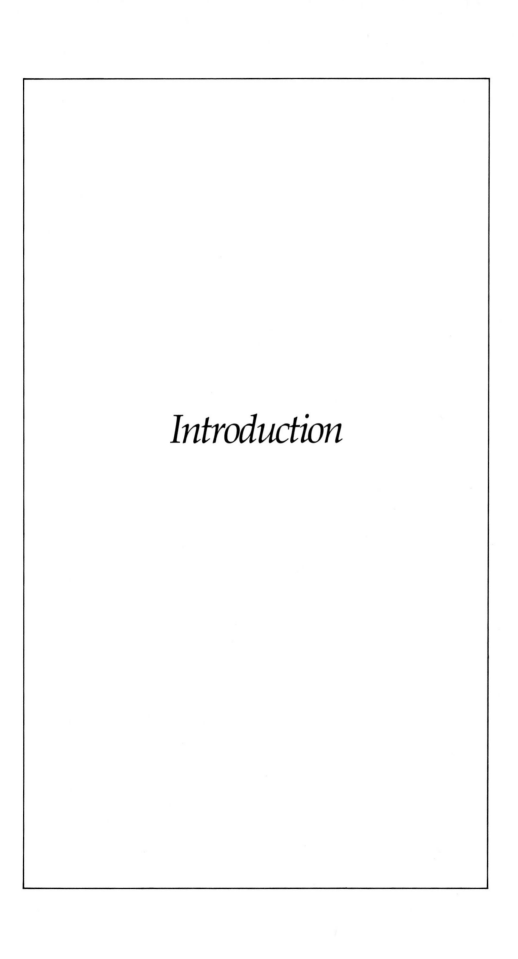

Introduction

The Canadian North Country of 1903 was as awesome, mysterious, gorgeously beautiful, and terribly thrilling to sportsmen as it is today. Little has been changed by the paramount of changers: accessibility.

Certainly, there are the float planes and there are modern camps, in contrast to the tent life of 75 years ago. There are excellent highways and there are snowmobiles and even house boats, but Northern Canada is a vast country and still very much an unspoiled frontier.

The basic fundamentals of life in this part of Canada remain relatively unchanged since Frank E. Schoonover first set foot here in 1903. During most of the year, the Indians still depend on their harvest of fur. The Hudson's Bay Company is still their depository, and it is flourishing.

Today as in years gone by, the methods of living and making a living are, for most months of the year, too difficult to be changed radically even by the concept of years and years of passing time. The Canadian North Country has always had a terrific magnetism for people of vital outdoor interests, and it offers much adventure not to be found elsewhere on the North American continent.

Frank E. Schoonover was drawn by this magnetism of adventure. He made several extended visits to Northern Canada in the early twentieth century, and painted and wrote from his experiences. His work reflected his fascination with the Canadian wilds throughout his life.

Schoonover was a man of great scope. He was a writer, a lecturer, and a well-respected artist who had studied under the renowned illustrator and teacher, Howard Pyle. He and other Pyle students, such as N. C. Wyeth, were part of an artistic coterie in what has been referred to as "the Golden Age of Illustration".

He is perhaps best remembered for the illustrations he created for such prominent writers as: Jack London (White Fang)*, John Buchan* (The House of the Four Winds)*, Sir Gilbert Parker* (The Lane that had no Turning *and* Northern Lights)*, W. A. Fraser* (The Blood Lilies)*, Constance Lindsay Skinner* (Roselle of the North)*, Rex Beach* (Where Northern Lights Come Down)*, Captain Frederick Marryat* (Masterman Ready)*, George Marsh* (Sled Trails and White Waters, Under Frozen Stars, The Valley of Voices, The Whelps of the Wolf)*, Robert W. Chambers* (Cardigan)*, Dillon Wallace* (Bobby of Labrador)*, and many other Canadian writers for whom he illustrated both books and magazine stories. Today, his original paintings are in the permanent collections of the Brandywine Museum, Chadds Ford, Pennsylvania, the Delaware Art Museum, Wilmington, and the Glenbow-Alberta Institute, Calgary.*

In addition, Schoonover remains one of the best photographers to record the rugged beauty of Canada during the early part of the century. About 800 of his Canadian photographic studies have survived, and their clarity of definition, as witness some of the reproductions in this book, is indeed remarkable. He was, in fact, one of the first photographers to use roll film in Canada and almost certainly one of the first to put roll film through the rigors of outdoor winter conditions.

1900 to 1915 was for Frank E. Schoonover a period of intense work on illustrations for Scribner's, McClure's, Century, Outdoor, and many other magazines which specialized in depicting the Canadian North Country. To gain authenticity for his painting, he set out in November 1903 on an extraordinary journey in Canada that took him some 1,200 miles by snowshoe and dogsled in the Hudson Bay and James Bay areas. He kept a faithful diary of this journey and accumulated an invaluable store of drawings and photographs.

Again in 1911, the artist made a major trip in this general area, but this time by canoe and portage during the spring and summer. On return, he was once more steeped in vast resources of additional experience and material for his store of Canadiana.

It was from these experiences that Schoonover brought, as one of his editors put it, ". . . the very breath and feeling of the big Canadian outdoors. His great Canadian adventures have proved the inspiration and the exact information that have made his truth-telling pictures possible."

It can be said that Frank E. Schoonover was faithful to the Canadian wilderness until the very end of his long active career (over 65 years) at the easel. Without question, Frank E. Schoonover's long, full life was characterized by a very virile outlook that always seemed to be filtering through the Canadian North Country scene. His last work was an easel painting (reproduced in this book) entitled "The Spirit of the Wendigo". It is fitting that this picture embodies a summation of what in his bright budget of memories highlighted his enthusiasm for the rugged strength of the Canadian North – the raw majesty which he lived and communicated so beautifully.

Part One

*From
the Day Book of
the Winter
Expedition of
1903-1904*

On December 24th, Christmas Eve, 1903, Frank E. Schoonover commenced entries in a diary as follows: "In this book, I purpose keeping a somewhat detailed account, with impressions, of a trip in the bush near Lake St. John, Quebec, Canada."

He was only 26 years old, but already a widely known illustrator of the Canadian wilderness. It was the special purpose of this 1903 winter expedition to enhance his background of authentic experience with the Canadian people and the Canadian country. And it was with this background, further bolstered by additional exploratory trips in the Hudson Bay, the James Bay, and Ungava Bay areas, that he became a popular illustrator for the true and exciting flavor of his illustrations of the Canadian wilderness.

It was 17 degrees below zero on December 18th, 1903, when the traveller reached Lac au Sable, a little village on the lake of the same name in the Province of Quebec. He and his two guides, Xavier Gill, a full-blooded Montagnais Indian, and his companion Skene, a half-breed, who had been "in training" for about a month in and about Cap Rouge near Quebec City, unloaded the little expedition's gear and provisions from the "petit" baggage car of the Great Northern train that had brought them from Rivière à Pierre.

Since it was too late in the afternoon to induce any carter to cart their luggage to Lac Brule some six miles off, they were on their own from here on. The highlights of the traveller's record are better stated in his own words.

Yes, it was only six miles off, but one man said his ox was too slow and he was afraid to take his horse over the bad roads in the dark. Besides his horse was somewhere in the bush! These people are absolutely too indifferent at times to take money when offered.

Nearly every house has its flag pole, with the top variously ornamented, usually by beaver, fish or deer running. The upper section of one has an elaborate ornament at the base consisting of four wooden guns placed with their butts at the corners of a platform and with their muzzles leaning against the pole. From the platform at each point hangs a chain and ball.

Xavier tells me the people put up all sorts of flags not knowing to what country they belong. They simply want the show and the color. Some use signs rather than flags. One of the signs was rather good, made to resemble a baker. It represented the cross section of a loaf of bread and the name "josselin" with the j and i dotted.

In the little boarding house where the two men and I suppered, slept and breakfasted, the ceilings of the two principal lower rooms were covered with the same pattern oil-cloth as the floor. This originates a new word, "oil-clothed" instead of papered!

We made an early start from Lac au Sable, barely able to see our way in the darkness of beginning dawn. The low, wood sleigh was loaded with tent, baggage, and 12 loaves of bread. These loaves are real French Canadian affairs that are double-barrelled and cost 15 cents.

For about a mile we walked the edge of Lac au Sable, a long irregular level of white, the bordering hills deep purple with a suggestion of crimson, and the sky a deep gray-yellow increasing in color as the sun rose. At intervals, the wind had blown the ice clear of snow and upon these areas one's moccasins held with a faint rasping-like rubbing of long grasses.

Leaving the lake, we followed for one or two hours a sparsely used wood road. In fact, had not the trees been blazed, any direction in the bush would have been a road to my unaccustomed eyes. Rough precipitation, full of stumps, with sides of a variance of three, four, likely even five feet high – these are a few details of a wood road.

In walking along (myself being the last of the brigade in order to secure the advantage of trodden snow), an idea of a story occurred. It was suggested by the remark of Xavier of how a trapper, the previous winter, caught two black foxes and, not knowing their value, sold the skins for $150 each, the true worth being anywhere from $700 to $1000.

I thought of calling such a story "The Black Fox". Perhaps the fox has been seen by several trappers and evades capture. Possibly

Xavier Gill, Schoonover's Indian guide, seated in interior of tent; 1903.
Photograph by F. E. Schoonover.

it is a form of the "Loup Sorrow" – possibly a myth. At any rate, it has the foundation of something good with the setting of those lakes and mountains!

Roads and paths appeared, breaking suddenly to the lakes. I was on the point of asking the remaining distance to Lac Brule when, without apparent difference in the land, the frozen, snow-covered surface of a large body of water appeared. Once in the open again, I noticed a considerable difference of temperature. While the cold was quite severe, the bush had broken the wind, but on the lake without the protection of the bush, the change was immediately worse. After a mile's walking, my feet, before perfectly warm, were stinging and my face was quite stiff from the cutting wind. A sharp turn of the lake brought the wind on our backs and so the remaining two miles were comparatively easy.

At one point, however, some danger was encountered in crossing the ice. Though it was of sufficient thickness, it seems true of all these northern lakes that a heavy snowfall causes the ice beneath to sink and at the same time forces the water to the surface. This process continues throughout the winter. A hole cut in the ice late in January or February will reveal first snow and slush, then ice and foam in successive layers for seven or eight feet or more. Thus, in certain places on the lake where some obstruction or protecting shore has prevented the wind from clearing the snow, one is liable to break through a thin layer of ice with a foot or more slush.

The driver waited while Xavier tested the passage across the · lake with his axe, and finally gave a favorable wave, starting with loud cries of "Marche donc."

A quarter after ten when the carter had tumbled off our last piece of provision, the sight of the camp was the southern point of Lac Brule (also called Lac François) and the southern shore.

After cutting away some brush and an old stump, Xavier, in Montagnais snowshoes, tramped the snow for about a twenty foot space and made a path that led to the lake. On this packed snow square, with tips toward the center, were laid spruce branches of five or six inches thickness, making the floor of the tent home. Over this square, the tent (dark brown with use and with patches in many places), supported by cross pieces at each end which held the ridge pole – all cut from spruce trees near the lake – was erected.

The bed which serves likewise as tables, chairs, general resting place, and storehouse on the sides occupies about three-fifths of the floor space. Some eight or ten logs, ends resting on cross pieces, were placed the entire width of the tent and upon these, layer after layer of spruce boughs were placed with double branches for security.

The stove, a folding sheet iron affair, is about two-and-a-half feet from the foot of this "bed" and is fully capable of either freezing or roasting one.

The tent was up, interior constructed, wood cut, two large birches felled, and dinner ready by two o'clock! All this done in less than four hours. By that time, I had caught a few trout through the ice, made a tour of the camping end of the lake, and felt fully able to enjoy some meat and potatoes dumped as a common article of food on a round tin plate. Like a true bushman, I attacked it with my bushman's knife and uttered the glutton's "bon bon" whenever I had a rest.

The day is officially over at about four o'clock. All members of the expedition, including the dogs, are in the tent for the evening, and it is then that one removes superfluous clothing, especially stockings. I was interested in watching Xavier taking off two pairs of his stockings and his mittens. He fastened the lot with a huge brass safety pin and hung them on the line running the length of the tent just beneath the ridge pole.

This, by the way, is a great place for almost everything. Soon, I was able to count some 21 items including a pair of low moccasins, stockings, a red sash, a black silk muffler, a clean towel, a pair of caribou mittens, two used towels, and Xavier's collection of wet socks and mittens. Next to Xavier's socks, and almost covered by them, came the cook's dish rag – hung to dry in happy company! At the end of the line was the dish mop, and below was the ever present pail of tea, which reminds me of a story I want to tell here.

It seems that in a bush camp late one evening one of the men got himself a cup of tea. He thought it had a peculiar taste but forgot the matter until the morning when one of the men, missing a sock from his bundle of stockings, started a hunt. The cook in making ready for breakfast found it in the tea pail!

No one sleeps the first night who is not accustomed to the life, but my guides seemed to get along very well in the early morning judging by the music and the babble of French Canadian.

January 12, 1904. Two degrees below zero and snowing in an uncertain way. The loads were about packed and ready when the dogs were found to be missing, probably chasing after a hare. Now here was an interesting state of affairs, since no dogs meant no moving. The guides circled the mighty camp, finding the tracks crossing and re-crossing. Finally they returned with our wayward power units. My wait, however, had been full of uncertain thoughts. I wondered what

Portrait of Xavier Gill, from Day Book of the Winter Expedition; 1903.
Pencil sketch.

to eliminate in reducing a load and just how possible it would be to pull 150 pounds and remain enthusiastic for the duration of the trip.

A stony ridge was discovered in an hour which at our rate of travel meant three miles. An Indian in the last village had told us that the trail led right across this ridge to a little river, then to a small lake and then to a larger one.

Here is the truth of the matter: "right across" was a good five miles, and very "good" to be sure! It was, however, just one of the many exasperating judgments of distance which I never really got used to in working with the casual Indians and which made it very hard for me to adjust the daily portions of the trip into reasonably proper camping stops.

At the end of this five miles was a long, hard portage. When we came to the end of it, it was ten o'clock – original dinner hour and we stopped for some eating and the blessed steaming tea which was our strength. This break was a remarkable restorative for the innocents who imagine bush walking in the bitter Canadian winter is fun. Let those who do, put on snowshoes and pack one load and pull another over a difficult portage. Let them have a fall as I did very early in the morning, straining the toes under the thongs of the snowshoes, and walking 18 miles by three o'clock with but two stops for food or drink!

At the end of our hard portage was a little river with a better trail and at its end, the first lake. Here we stopped for some tea and hardtack and a bit of rest. The dogs were getting tired, increasing my work. The little (so called by the Indians) lake was a good mile long. It was crossed and recrossed by fox tracks. At one place it was very evident a poor hare had been chased. His jumps were prodigious, while those of the fox ran even and deadly alongside.

We could not make it to the big lake so we camped. I am beginning to understand preparations for the night. I don't think I ever appreciated more the comforts of a bed on the snow than tonight. Eighteen miles of hard walking and working on snowshoes makes any sort of shelter a comfort and the food a luxury. Tonight we had flapjacks fried in the pan, and syrup made of melted cake maple molasses. Such things taste as such things never tasted before, and I fear I indulged too heavily, for they were weighty!

January 13, 1904. Three degrees above zero and still moderating after a night of stillness and quiet. We left our camp at about eight and made the lake, the big one, in about an hour. This magnificent body of water was three miles long. About halfway the length, we stopped at an old Indian camp. Still resting on its four posts was the small stove, dilapidated, and useless. Hanging on a tree was a broken iron kettle, and on another tree at about eight feet from the ground was a string of boxes, 18 rabbit skulls, and the wing bones of a loon.

Xavier tells me that stringing the bones of the animals is a common custom of the Indians. These startling remnants are put up for good luck. Sometimes they are hung by a piece of caribou or string, sometimes they are strung on a branch. A bear head is honored more than the others, always having a separate stake of its own. A piece of plug tobacco is put in the nostril socket. If an Indian happens to be without anything to smoke and sees a bear's head on its stake, he is sure of some tobacco unless, of course, another impoverished Indian has preceded him!

At the extreme end of the long Lac la Lontre (Otter Lake) we left the Indian trail. This necessitated the making of a new one and this is the hardest, most tiresome work possible in the bush. Toboggans were left on the lake, and with one of the guides breaking trail with the wide snowshoes, we tramped snow, cut trees and bush for a mile-and-a-half and then had to go back for the loads.

After dinner, we broke trail again, this time for three miles until darkness came upon us. Tired, footsore, faces burning from the branches – for us, work continued, for we had camp to make, wood to cut, water to be carried, and all this in a heavy snow storm, before a cup of hot tea could be had and a place made ready to rest. After such a day, the comforts of a tent, the fire, and the soundness of sleep flat on the snow (the latter less and less cold every night as one becomes accustomed) are most appreciated rewards.

The fire is kept alive all night long for our comfort and for the dogs.

These beasts are a wonder to me in regard to the stove. The stove, a thin sheet, gets red hot continually, and if one of the dogs is asleep too close to it, we are reminded by the odor of burning hair.

I think it very likely we shall have to keep this camp over tomorrow. Trail must be made for a day's journey of nine-and-one-half miles and nothing can be gained by short movements of the camp.

January 14, 1904. The temperature is still moderating and when we got up at five o'clock it was six degrees above zero. We had breakfast at six in a very heavy snow which had been falling all night, but after the meal we still put out the fire very carefully. A small pack was made of frying pan, three cups, one small pail, three pieces of fat pork, some sugar and salt. We then set off for the hardest day of our travels. Each one of us had to carry an axe and Skene carried an axe and a gun. We labored north by west, hard in the face of the terrible storm which badly handicapped us. It was impossible to see past a short distance, and I had to rely entirely on the compass. We had no advantage of the directions from the mountains, and it was a hard trail to cut through tangles of bush and heavy snow.

About a mile from camp we started a portage and saw a partridge still asleep in the little snow house they make for the night. It flew but a few feet when Skene killed it and another bird whose head was just protruding from the snow. This seemed a cruel means of hunting, but after five days on pork, such incriminating thoughts came only after eating the birds – not before!

Undoubtedly, these were four hours of the hardest walking I ever hope to experience! At eleven o'clock when I stopped the men, we had made a passable eight miles of trail through a hitherto un-travelled country. We were the first and I hope none will follow, especially under the conditions we were subjected to. I was trying not to show it, but I was truly bone-tired and footsore to the limit. Another fall had added to my difficulty in walking. Even the Indians admitted they had never seen worse and that they had never believed they could make such going. At this, I felt somewhat comforted for I attributed much of my suffering to my lack of experience and knowledge of the country.

Since there was no water available we melted snow to make tea, cooked the two birds with the pork, and ate like true inhabitants of the bush!

The river which we were seeking – the Vermillion – had not been reached by this point, nor was there any sign of a river. I sent the men on with the hope of their making trail through, and I returned to our camp, making the eight miles in two hours. Never did any place seem more welcome than the tent, although it presented a most forsaken appearance. Everything was snow-covered. I made a fire, brought in a large pail of water (that in the tent was frozen solid) and soon had some tea. Then I melted some maple sugar, refried some of last night's flapjacks and feasted.

About two hours later, the men returned and disheartened me with a very disturbing fact. It seemed that because of the truly blinding nature of the storm, we had travelled north by east, in fact almost northeast instead of north by west. As far as the small lake being about six miles from the camp, the direction was due north, but beyond that, the day's hard work was for nothing. Tomorrow a fresh road must be made from the lake.

We are all very tired and quiet tonight. Even the dogs were asleep without calling for their pancakes. I felt the wind colder somehow, and I imagine tomorrow will be a stinging day.

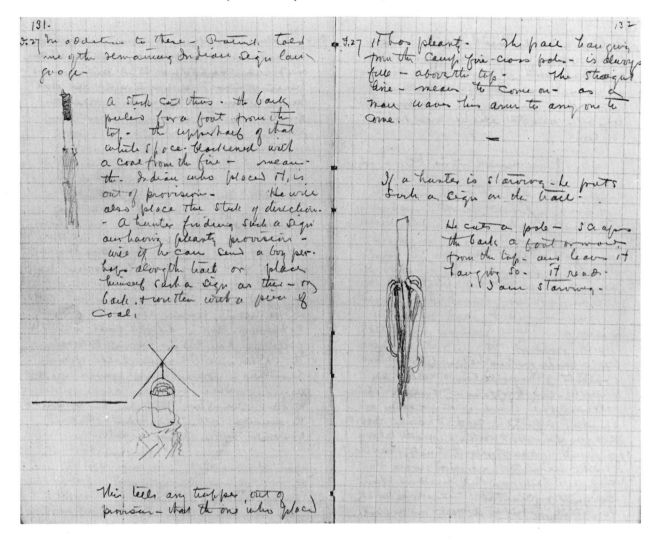

In an entry of the Day Book, Schoonover explains and illustrates Indian signs used in the wilderness: (1) A specially prepared stick indicates that someone in the area is out of provisions. The stick is placed so that it points to his location. (2) An overflowing pail of trash indicates that the one who has hung it has plenty of provisions. The stick on the ground shows the direction of his location. (3) A pole with its bark peeled back indicates that someone ahead is starving.

January 15, 1904. We were a little late in getting started this morning because although it was only 15 degrees below zero and clear a very strong cold wind was blowing and making it extremely difficult to break camp and pack our gear. The late start was just as well, for we were already exhausted by noon.

What a cold, cold, bitter cold country this is. With the fierce wind from the northwest freezing one's face, I had to rub my face, cheeks and nose, again and again to keep them from actually freezing. The greater part of the morning, I walked with one hand protecting my face.

Before starting, I had purposely drunk more tea than I wanted, hoping to store some for the unbelievably hard walk; but scarcely an hour had passed before I was hungry and thirsty. Drinking on the trail is impossible unless one stops to make tea. Cold water is fatal as one grows weak from it immediately.

A complete change of weather shortly after the middle of the day made this the most picturesque afternoon of all – the most perfectly clear, though very cold, weather and fine color. We seemed to be making a portage over a height of land almost full of small bush. Clusters of pines dotted the ridges, and beyond the mountains a deep purple developed, increasing as the afternoon sun gave more and more color. The level of the snow, vividly pink now in the setting sunlight, was in sharp contrast to any shadows, for they were an intense blue purple. Later, when the light came from the afterglow, the western sky was rich in a color of red to gray yellow. High above the horizon was a deep, somewhat cold yellow. This deepened to a red-yellow and to a broad orange red. Against this, cutting sharp, the pines were almost black – a deep green purple brown – the immediate sweep of snow a pink purple with an intervening hill a deep blue purple.

January 18, 1904. 30 degrees below zero this morning with the sure prospects of a terrible day of cold that would be doubly cold (in the neighborhood of 55 or 60 degrees below zero – a cold so severe that the freezing trees sound off like rifle shots) on the river. We had reached the Vermillion the day before and had camped the night at the two portages on a little height overlooking the river. How cold the tent had seemed during this awful night. Even the stove seemed against us, the pipe becoming choked with the resinous soot of the cypress. Although we hade made a good nine miles on the 17th, we shall have to remain here a day at least.

Cold as it is, though, I shall put up my little house on the river and make a sketch of it and the open water of the rapid. I had the men put up my sketching house very near the open water. What a unique sight, miles away from any civilized community and in the very wild of the North on a frozen river to see an Indian struggling in the nerve-testing icy wind with an artist's sketching tent.

Holes for the uprights and stakes were cut in the ice, and when they had been placed in position water was poured around their bases. In a few minutes, the whole structure was perfectly rigid. Next, the canvas was placed, well tied, and the window with panes covered with a solution of glycerin and high wine was slipped into place. The stove was put in the doorway, all in the killing temperature of 49 below.

So cold were our hands and faces that we rubbed them with snow. By ten in the morning, we were using energy so fast that we had to stop and return to camp for dinner. The men left shortly after the big meal, however, and went to work breaking trail and carrying 100 pounds of flour some five miles up the lake.

It was twelve o'clock when I started the fire in the stove in the sketching tent and commenced drawing. The whole procedure was so novel, original, and seemingly impossible that I stopped for a moment later in the day and photographed the tiny house. The three-and-a-half hours spent in that terrible windy day of horrible cold with the window facing due north by west were a sure test of the practicality of the tent. And practical it was, if one only considers personal comfort sufficiently warm to work without gloves or extra coat. In fact, I found almost any degree of heat could be obtained simply by pulling in or pushing out the stove. I worked until the men returned about the falling of light, gathered up my materials, put on snowshoes, and trailed back to camp — the first of all illustrators (so far as I know) to pack a sketching house through the bush by dog train and carry his work to the tent home while walking on snowshoes!

January 21, 1904. Since the 18th, we had made little progress, actually only a total of six miles. Many factors had worked against us. For one thing, the unbelievable severity of the cold which never got above 40 degrees below zero took a terrible and unusually unpredictable toll on all of us and our equipment. The rubber bulb on my camera froze. In trying to thaw it, I froze one of my fingers. Thawing out a finger is no easy matter, and I had to stop to do it. The pack train had to go on, however, and when I finally got my finger working, my men were far ahead.

Instead of following the beaten trail around the curve of the river, I made strange cuts through the snow which had become very

Schoonover and his sketching tent; 1903.

Schoonover's Winter Camp; 1903.
Photograph by F. E. Schoonover.

Skene holds frying pan over smoke pipe to prevent sparks from setting fire to the brush.

deep. I overtook the men in time but at the cost of lacerated toes as I found out later. The guides had suffered too, even accustomed as they are to the northern winter. The unusual severity of the wind combined with the awful cold had surprised them. Both of Skene's ears and cheeks were frozen. Xavier had wrapped an American flag about his face so the stars and stripes had protected him. I had managed only with my fur cap pulled well down, a large silk handkerchief about the cap, a Hudson's Bay capote hood over all, and one hand over my nose!

Another factor that nearly destroyed us was the fact that at this point in the trip we had to make a mile-long portage over a mountain to Lac aux Branches. Xavier warned me that this was the second worst portage in the eastern country, second only to one between the Vermillion River at Pointe Bleue and Lake Mistassini. All three of us and the dogs had to pull and push at the loads, gaining ground by inches only, and sometimes losing by feet. All of us at times lost foothold and slid down the slopes, making the going so difficult that we had to discontinue all thought of movement after the night of the 20th.

We had to keep active, however, and I made my men load my sketching house, stove, wood, and materials back to the worst bit of the portage. I surprised myself by being able to sketch for a few hours. During this time, the men made a bit of trail ahead, but spent most of the time setting traps and making the camp more comfortable. I had not produced much (simply had not been able to make my fingers move enough) in the way of a sketch, so I decided to stay over another day and try to finish one piece of work at least. While I worked, I could hear trees cracking. Xavier says (contrary to some of my former statements) that green balsam never cracks, that only pine and cypress do. Regardless, it was so cold this day the whole of the woods sounded like one live battleground!

How queer my little tent must have appeared from up the hill – an artist's sketching house on a footpath, travelled but twice a year by an Indian and family. I was a parasite, if you please, in the primeval Canadian forest!

It's rather odd, working like this, handling a stove from a snowbank, making fire, piling wood inside the tent, sliding in the window, and then between tending fire and rubbing the frost from the window glass doing a little art work while it is 45 degrees below zero outside. Actually, I was very comfortable, making myself as warm as I wished simply by pulling the stove a little closer.

Skene said my sketching house reminded him of those used by the medicine men, the conjurors of the Montagnais. He said they place many heavy posts in a circular shape to a considerable depth in the ground. Birch bark is fastened around the posts, and a small hole is left at the top.

The medicine man of the tribe enters this finished structure, and a drum is hung high above his head – too high for an ordinary man. The *cabane* is closed and the conjuror begins a kind of monotone accompanied by the impressive beats of the drum. When the Indian has worked himself into a frenzied state, a condition of almost utter exhaustion, he foretells the future, little or great, according to the remuneration previously agreed upon.

This brings to mind a true story of conjuring told me by an old Hudson's Bay factor. It was summer at Ungava, the far northern part of Labrador, and the men were awaiting the Hudson's Bay Company supply ship which touched this post but once a year. The usual time of its arrival had passed by a week or two, and the factor became anxious about his winter provisions. A friend staying with him suggested they give the medicine man some money and ask him to conjure. He did. After the weird performance, he issued from the tent and said he had seen the ship, but it had turned about very near the bay and was disappearing. He also said that on the forward deck he had seen a strange arrival, a new kind of creature to him and one he knew nothing about. So much for the magic spell! Winter and the spring passed. Summer brought the ship and the explanation that a year ago they had found the entrance to the factor's bay blocked with ice and had to turn back. On board, the English captain told them, had been an English stag hound, a present to the factor at Ungava!

It commenced snowing at about two o'clock so I finished what I could do on the sketch and made for camp. At the time of my writing (about eight) a hard storm blows. Xavier thinks it doubtful if we can move in the morning. I think otherwise!

January 23, 1904. We awoke to a heavy snow which almost covered the broken trail of the day before. We experienced many annoying delays including a frozen tent, a bad runner on one of the sleighs, and a broken thong on one of my foot coverings. This thong had to be thawed out before I could repair it. And repaired it had to be, because even slightly damaged equipment can be dangerous on the trail in the extreme cold. As a consequence of these annoyances, we made a late start.

The day was one of making trail and bringing along the toboggans. The sixteen wapoo traps between the two portages had not been touched because the night had been too stormy.

Breaking trail in deep snow while it is still snowing is exhausting work and we had to give in to the forces of nature and make camp early. When we had set up for the night, Xavier began saying negative things about an owl hooting near the tent. He was very talkative for some reason, perhaps because he was annoyed with the noisy bird. "More snow," Xavier said. "We no like owl to keep hooting at us, but he never fail tell you right about more snow."

Xavier also told me of a superstition the Indians have about the St. Maurice River. This has to do with a certain rapid called "the Devil (Wendigo) Rapids". To the Indians, the water is a source of great fear. Occasionally, they believe, an old man appears, swimming about in the water, attempting to catch them. The *voyageurs* rush through, lest their canoe be overturned. Strangely, because of this and other superstitions, fear makes the Indian a poor swimmer. I use the word "strangely" because the Indian lives his life in the environment of water – the Canadian North Country streams, small rivers, lakes, ponds, and muskegs both open and frozen. It makes me think of the old adage about sailors who can't swim!

Skene tells another story. During a long drive in the spring, he and two others were coming through a rapid, falling on an occasional log. They were in a boat, not a canoe, and near the foot of the rapid a large spruce log, caught midway across another log, swung around, striking the boat at the stem and overturning it. One of the men was never heard of again.

At another time, in a logging camp, a number of men (about 50) had been placed along a series of rapids which terminated in a waterfall of some height. During the week the logs ran well. Saturday night they jammed. Sunday the men were ordered out to break the log jam, which they did rather reluctantly. But it so happened that on Saturday night, after another week of free running, the logs blocked again at the head of the falls, and the men, as before, were ordered to work on Sunday. The first Sunday of extra work was bad enough, but on the second they felt queer about it, saying someone would be killed working on a Sunday. Rather than work again on Sunday, 20 of the men left.

January 24, 1904. We had a much better start this morning. We got up at half past four, had breakfast, packed our train, and were off at seven. At the time, I thought how few people at home were up and walking at that hour!

To gain time and make a better day, I made trail myself most of the morning and *all* the afternoon. This was done not only to gain a few miles, but to experience and feel the utter exhaustion of such work. After dinner at eleven in the morning, I was more than a mile ahead of the men. This gradually decreased, however, as the day wore on. The men appeared to be nothing more than black spots far away. swinging slowly, steadily – without any apparent stop – but with the sure walk of years of experience and training on snowshoes. I, however, with false determination would start, make a few yards, then take a brief rest during which I would take a look back. I continued thus for three-and-a-half hours. Proceeding thus, I naturally found the men catching up on me in the afternoon.

I often wondered what the men thought throughout the day. Usually, I imagined they thought about little or nothing, concentrating on the difficult job of keeping on a fairly straight course. I came to learn, however, that when their minds did wander off the trail, they tended to remember great hunts and great adventures that built up over the years.

Xavier, who kept immediately behind me at the end of the day, finally waved his hand and said, "Camp – le gros cypres." This indicated the night's camp some distance away near three tall cypresses. The snow at this part of the river was the heaviest and deepest of the day. Snowshoes would sink further and further. Then, the pounds of snow that fell in over the snowshoes at each step, plus the ice that had accumulated on our footwear during the day, had to be lifted by muscles that had been calling for rest an hour before!

With a clean, unbroken record as lead man for the afternoon, I made the three tall trees and said, "Bon." The end of the day brought a little new strength, however, so I hung my camera, loosened my axe, and made my share of the camp. The day had been clear and mild up to the time of our nearing the camping place. As we stopped, the wind began blowing the snow in from places among the trees along the mountain top. Before camp was made, a biting snow and wind storm enveloped us and the temperature fell to 25 below zero. This was going to be a cold night for sure, but for me, all the better, because I sleep more successfully on a really cold night than on one at a mild five or ten below zero!

January 25, 1904. The snow of last night amounted to nothing. The howling wind left only very cold air (and harder snow, I trust). The men broke trail by alternate turns. It was too much for me to break trail today, particularly as the river is full of rapids. The portages around them are no easy matter, for there is often a question of the ice bridges holding. Once during the morning, while leading, I suddenly broke through an ice bridge and had the novel sensation

23

of being suspended above a roaring rapid. Fortunately, my arms caught, and the men hauled me out. We proceeded as though nothing had happened. Here is a question: I wonder how one fares going through the ice with snowshoes?

We made a big portage at noon. By the time the men brought the dogs and sleds over, I had a fire going, and in a very few minutes tea and pork were ready. I was also toasting some frozen "gillets" and my hands over the fire.

I had made the fire against a great tall dead tamarack. It occurred to me: why not a story told by a tamarack? It might be called "The Song of the Tamarack". Here is a tree that has seen the first of the Indians, then the *courrier de bois*, soon the Jesuit fathers, followed closely by the Hudson's Bay Company factors, their enemies the free traders, the French *voyageurs*, trappers, hunters, and lastly death from the forest fire.

There is a very picturesque spirit surrounding this particular camp so we shall probably remain here tomorrow. I will put the little sketching tent up on the river somewhere nearby. Unbelievably, it is getting colder with a quiet but bold persistence that seems to penetrate everything and everyone. We all like the stove and the dogs this evening, I notice! At eight o'clock in the evening, I checked the temperature and found it to be 40 below zero just outside the tent flap. A little later I checked again and it had dropped almost to 50 degrees below zero. I did not check again, but by morning I think the wind will slack and the temperature will moderate. Fortunately it does not stay as cold as 50 degrees below zero for too long at a stretch.

January 26, 1904. While Xavier was cooking some pork, Skene and I put up my tent on the river at the foot of a rapids. Xavier came down to inspect it, as his pork was nearly ready and both men seemed doubtful about the safety of the outfit, but for the sake of art and considering how very cold it was, I put more than ordinary faith in the ice.

It was still very cold despite my hopes of moderation in the temperature and we decided on an early dinner because we needed strength against the terrible cold. The men could not just hang around while I painted so they forced themselves to break trail for the next day and I finished my sketch before dark.

Again, for art's sake and for the maintenance of the mechanics of life, I carried to my sketching tent that afternoon a pail of tea and a cup. There may be very little difference between half-tones and high-lights, but always a cup of tea!

Height of Land Portage; 1904.
Crayon; 11 x 17.

Trapper with Christmas Tree; 1923.
Oil; 25 x 36.

On the Asawan; 1904.
Crayon; 11 x 17.

Breaking Trail; 1924.
Oil; 26 x 48.

Snowblind; 1914.
Oil; 32 x 40.

With the Winter Mail; 1917.
Oil; 24 x 36.

Three Faces in the Tent; 1904.
Oil; 12 x 14.

I had not worked long before the ice directly beneath me began cracking. For safety's sake, I placed my camera and snowshoes (my two essentials) on the shore and tried the ice with my axe. I decided to continue working; the cracking also continued. What with the open water, the rumbling of the water, the cracking of ice beneath, and the blowing of the wind above, I had rather queer sensations!

February 2, 1904. Yesterday, after an incredible period of the most bitter cold and cruel winds, we had awakened to find it had warmed to 15 degrees below zero and the change so inspired us that, walking from seven until five, we accomplished what the Indians said was impossible, we covered 21 miles! This was achieved despite the fact that one of the dogs gave out sometime in the forenoon (our noon being eleven o'clock), and from then on, I pushed the load, while the dog made a brave but feeble effort to pull. We were further inspired because we had a specific destination, the Hudson's Bay Company Post at Pointe Bleue. We had experienced such excruciating cold for what had seemed an inescapable eternity that I was perhaps more glad than the men, when the trail finally merged into a lumberman's wood road some three miles from the Post. As we drew nearer and nearer to respite from the bush, excitement seized the group, snowshoes were slipped, and we ran with the dogs – a mile and a half to the first dwelling!

The warmth of the hospitality of the Canadian North Country just has to be experienced to be believed. I am going to accept some rest here, and draw and photograph and try to translate the unfettered joy that our visit seems so genuinely to have created.

February 10, 1904. We left the Post on February 9th, having been persuaded to spend a final night at the Post in a shack where, upon entering, I found a pig under process of dissection on the table which later was cleared for the supper and our eating. I was informed that such butchering was not always the custom, but the weather being so cold it was better to work in the house.

The accommodations in a house of this sort are such as one makes. Use of the stove for cooking and the table to eat upon are the only gratuitous services. For myself and men, Xavier brought inside the cooking utensils, tea, pork, biscuits, and some caribou. After the family had finished, the table and stove were left for our use. Breakfast was handled in the same fashion. As for sleeping, the men spread their blankets on the floor, and I bought the use of a bed for the night!

Day Book entry and portrait of Semo-Mac-Me-Call and his brother; 1904.
Pencil sketch.

Semo (the lower) and his brother.
In my tent. Wednesday afternoon.
They were talking with J. + not posing.

Rather late in the evening at this place – about eight – a driver from the logging camp entered and without much talk and less ceremony seated himself at the table, unwrapped a tin plate filled with cold pork and a piece of bread and made his supper. He asked for a cup of tea, and in payment left the approximate quantity in the raw state. This, too, became our custom the following day at a lumber camp.

Although this camp was not too far from the Post, it was extremely enervating to battle the very deep cold and high wind which had returned to the area. It took us all day to cover just a few miles, and that with the benefit of the outline, in the heavy snow, of a woods road.

Although this logging operation held the reputation of being the largest we would encounter, it had but one shanty, and that not very large, in which we found 20 men. But despite the crowding, we enjoyed their genuine hospitality. Unfortunately, however, no amount of body heat nor even a fire could prevent the penetration of this night's cold into a shanty. But amazingly enough, after a supper of nothing but beans, the men played cards for matches – this after their prayers said in response to a leader who intoned after the manner of a *curé*.

The sleeping was sound, even if the arrangements were distinctively primitive. Man alternated with dog flat on the floor – the men fully clothed with all layers of warm things they could find, and a pitiful assortment of blankets, mostly used under rather than over the sleeper!

February 11, 1904. The camp awakens early, the cook at four, and the choppers having a considerable distance to walk leave at six. I watched them from the camp: a small file of five or six in the cold pale yellow of the morning, winding up the wood road, swinging their axes in time to a song – a fine opportunity for a picture and a poem, brutal in its cutting rhythm, embodying the idea of the death of the dead forest, a forest where life already has been sapped and licked by the fire; a forest existing only as a symbol, the single standing death of its once green life.

February 12, 1904. Twenty degrees below zero, but the finest day of the year. The color is perfect and clear, and it is mild and quiet – a reward, surely, for all our hard days of walking. We made 13 miles on the La Croche to the winter home of Patrick Cleary. A late start and rather indifferent walking of the men, undoubtedly due to the

Toboggan followed by dog and sled; 1904.
Photograph by F. E. Schoonover.

Note the similarity between the painting and the photograph.

A Rest on the Trail; 1905.
Mechanical reproduction of oil painting.

improved weather, made a long day. It was half past five and growing quite dark when we reached the two or three log cabins that
comprised this trapper's modern camp.

Strangely, there was no sign of life. Obviously from the lack
of prints in the snow, he had gone elsewhere with his people. When
the men looked about, they found a letter, left for just such disappointed people as ourselves, saying that the families had left for
the month of February to try the hunting at another of his camps
about two days' away on the La Tranche River. We had to stay here
until the men could bring up the provisions and go on the two days'
journey.

February 13, 1904. Today, it got up to zero! I had expected to spend
this day in a general "catching up" in my writing, but at about noon
a half-breed Indian, his brother, and their dogs arrived. He was a
trapper hunting about two days' trail from here. He proved an interesting man who impressed me more favorably than any I have met
in the bush. He speaks French, Montagnais, and English. While we
were together, he told me some interesting things about his hunting.

Once, while coming along the river with his wife from the spring
hunt, they met a young bear swimming across the river. It seems
that the Indian crossed the bear's direction of swimming and the
animal turned upon them. His wife wanted to shoot, but the Indian
forced the canoe backwards, and the bear swam onto the shore
where the Indian killed him. The half-breed also told me of the best
day's hunting he had ever had. It seems that one day during the fall,
very near the camp, he shot two otters (*lutra canadensis*) from his
canoe. For these he received $44.

He also told me a rather long story about the death of his first
child, a boy. I note only the main facts: the boy was about nine
months' old when he and his wife left Pointe Bleue for the fall hunt.
They had left the logging camp some two days before and were well
along the trail toward his camp, when the little fellow sickened and
died. The father made a cache of some provisions, wrapped the body
in the tent and, with his wife, started the return. The second day,
the wife became very ill, travelling as they had in the rain. They
kept on, however, and finally made the village. He said he never
passes over that trail – never goes by that one place in the woods –
without feeling sick and bad.

"It's not so much now," he said, "but two or three years ago,
it was hard for me to make a hunt because it was so bad to go over
that trail."

February 16, 1904. It has dropped down to 15 below zero again during the warmest part of the day, but we managed to reach the log cabin of Patrick Cleary who prides himself as a hunter. He draws quite a difference between a hunter and a trapper. In the latter category, he places the French Canadians, the *habitants* and those younger woodsmen who can, by trapping, catch such animals as the mink, marten, lynx, and rabbit. They know the construction of the simple traps, the use of the dead-fall, and the more modern steel contrivances. But when the finer and more subtle faculties of trapping are necessary, such as the ability to place a heavy "keg and trap" by sense of feeling only, these trappers are at a loss. They find such fur-bearing animals beyond their cunning.

The hunter, however, is all that the trapper is and far more. To the hunter's smaller game must be added the larger – the caribou, moose, bear, the trapping of the otter, the beaver, and the fisher – and he must have a superior woods knowledge that enables him to take any kind of game.

Patrick was fascinated most by the challenge of the beaver. His custom was to build two kegs or barrels in the two passage ways leading into the beaver house. It is only when the alleyways are large and wide across, that these kegs are constructed; otherwise only a trap is set. The bait used is red birch and bitter poplar if it can be acquired. A beaver and his whole family will leave a lake and their house if they discover or even detect the odor of dead meat or the presence of a human being! This, of course, only refers to the open months, for once the ice is formed it becomes impossible for them to leave their houses, except to swim under the ice which keeps them prisoners of their little lakes. Once this ice forms (and it can quickly freeze the lake right down to the bottom), the cunning hunter must test his greatest skills to catch the beaver by cutting holes through the ice to set the traps. And how does he tell if the beaver has even been attracted to his bait? Well, he relies on bubbles – it's as simple as that! When the hunter checks his trap hole, it is frozen, of course. But if he sees bubbles in the ice, then he knows there has been activity.

On page 165 of the diary, the record of this extraordinary expedition gave way to the artist's intense devotion of his time, apart from travelling and just surviving, to drawing by day and night, until by the end of the late spring he had virtually all the attitudes of the Canadian North winter and its people drawn and redrawn, photographed and rephotographed, and driven and redriven into his memory.

Part Two

From the Day Book of the Summer Expedition of 1911

Frank Schoonover was such a devoted fisherman that his preoccupation with trout transcended even the most mature concept of fishing.

During his Canadian expedition in the winter of 1903-1904, trout had kept him and his men from starvation when his provisions ran out toward the end of the trip. It had been so cold that the animals ceased their movement, and he and his fellow travellers were prevented from finding even a little meat for sustenance.

By 1911, Schoonover had become famous for his portrayal of the Canadian North through his painting, photography, writing, and lecturing. His success had enabled him to become the owner of stretches of two great trout streams.

Today, the magnificent fishing in Canada is much more accessible than it was at the turn of the century, so the irresistible desire of the busy artist for an unhurried period of enjoyment in the Canadian fishing paradise had to be combined with a more practical pursuit, that of pursuing new subject matter for his paintings. Thus, he could enjoy the beauties of the Canadian summer, while at the same time supplying new enticements to his many publishers.

A summer expedition was planned. During his long winter in the Hudson Bay area in 1903 and 1904, he had lived with the hunters and trappers while they gathered their furs. Now, he would go back again and live the return of the fur-harvesters. He would portray their journey from the bush, the streams, and the lakes in their canoes laden with the gorgeous and fabulously valuable skins that would be fashioned to grace and warm the fastidious of a world which the fur-harvesters would never know and in which they could not exist.

By the time "F.E.", as he was coming to be known, had finally confirmed his plans, the expedition had been extended. For one thing, he had married. To enlist the enthusiasm of his new wife in his Canadian adventure, he planned for her, her sister, and some friends a delightful shopping and travelling trip through the provinces of Canada, a trip on which he was able to accompany her for part of the time.

The two sections of the expedition took their separate ways, however, very early in the morning of June 2, 1911 when "F.E." boarded train 97 of the Canadian Pacific Railway at Toronto and was soon on his way to his rail destination, Jackfish, a small village at the uppermost extreme of Lake Superior.

June 3, 1911. Our first view of the nearby country from the train was at 7:10 in the morning. To me, it was already very exciting although all we saw at the very beginning were barren rocks, some small lakes and a few streams. Later, in the middle of the morning, we were passing more vegetation, less rocks, but some burnt-over country, many more small lakes, and small streams of amber colored water.

At Chapleau, where we stopped for ten minutes, we saw some Indians. One Indian woman wore a dull red shirt and skirt. All wore moccasins of the high Cree type and with ornaments.

At Jackfish, I had immediate good luck. Fred Armstrong, a Canadian recommended as a prince of a canoe-man by the Hudson's Bay Post factor at Long Lake, and John Murphy, a burly Irish cook who was also a fine canoe-man from the same area, were cheerfully on hand to welcome me and to help with the unloading of my canoe and all my special gear which had been stowed so carefully in the baggage car.

It did not take us long with the help of a carter who brought us to Mountain Lake which Fred and John had picked as our starting point and where we immediately packed the canoe and were off.

All this happened very early in the morning of June 3, for we had crossed Mountain Lake and arrived at the portage called "Hell's Delight" by 7:20 in the morning. "Hell's Delight" portage joins Mountain Lake with Devil Lake. As we left Mountain Lake, I noticed two teepees of the Wendigo, the evil spirit of the Indians, and should have been warned of dangerous waters ahead. The portage over "Hell's Delight" was by far the worst of the trip, especially for me, even though Fred and John did most of the work.

A story prevails that one time a company of Indians was passing this point, when the Wendigo showed his anger with them by dropping a great piece of the mountain on their canoes, destroying all — papooses, squaws, braves, and their possessions.

Today when passing this point, it is customary to throw tobacco — at least one good big plug — into the water to appease the spirit of the Wendigo. And this is exactly what we did!

The beginning of the trip was quite an initiation for me. I packed my own duffel weighing at least 60 pounds over all the portage and then travelled 35 miles across Devil Lake to Moose Bogan Pond where we made camp at nine in the evening. There was still plenty of light in this far North Country.

June 4, 1911. Although there had been no opportunity for fishing on "breaking-in" day, I let out a trawl soon after we started out at 6:30

in the morning and caught a wall-eyed pike. I had another on the line a little later, but he must have been a very big one for he took spoon and line with him.

During this time, a fair wind began blowing and I abandoned my fishing to help rig a sail which we stretched across two birch poles. In the planning stage of this expedition, I had procured a large piece of bright red silk just for this sail as I knew it would help us with some of the long, hard paddling. It will also print a colorful picture in my mind for future reference in a painting or two.

Wind is fickle, of course, and this fair wind from the south shifted over to the east in about an hour. We had to take the sail down and paddle, resting for about five minutes each hour, until we reached the end of Steel Lake at about four in the afternoon. All of us rested and Fred went to sleep. We had covered 30 miles during this day.

We were now in the Long Lake trapping district and there were evidences of Indian camps – pieces of bark tents, big old pails, and some discarded moccasins. These evidences drove us on hard because they were a sign that we were behind some fur bearers on their way to Long Lake Post with their winter catch, and we wanted to be at the Post when they came in.

Our big push took us across many lakes – Bannock, Barmock, Eagle Rock, Pickerel, Green Water, McKay, and Granite Rock – before reaching Long Lake. Increasingly, as we approached Long Lake, we came across the remnants of the Indians. Much of their winter paraphernalia had been cached. On the shore of Green Lake, we inspected one of these caches. All the items left for use in the next season had been carefully wrapped and placed in a birch bark canoe which was suspended between two trees, and, of course, bottom up several feet above the ground.

In front of the canoe was a "lock" which consisted of a pole placed across the same two trees but above the canoe. This pole served as a sign to other passing Indians that the materials cached were wanted again. They were not bothered. This was the Savage Code of Honesty. The Indians who had constructed this cache had but recently built another canoe. Shavings lay among pieces of roots from the black spruce and balsam, with which they sew the bark together. In olden times, the Indians used spruce gum entirely to seal the seams, but now they obtain pitch from the Hudson's Bay Company. The canoes built by the Indians are about 14 feet long, wide of beam and deep.

There was an old sled for winter use propped against a tree, hung from which were also a black moose hide, snowshoes, 12

Bringing canoes to the water; 1911.
Lantern slides by F. E. Schoonover.

mittens made from an old Hudson's Bay Company blanket, and a boy's coat made from the same material.

Near the water, the Indians had constructed a small landing place, the logs of which were securely covered with spruce boughs – still green. Nearby was an old toboggan, but it must have been discarded like an old piece of farm machinery, although the bow had been painted green and red, maybe at Christmas time last year. Looking at the spruce boughs on the landing, Fred told me of how the Indians shade their eyes in winter with cedar boughs to prevent snow blindness. The cedar boughs are flat and spread out like a fan. I told Fred how I had used birch bark as a similar shield – narrow slits being cut in the bark. We both agreed that something better than any currently known protection was needed, because snow blindness was very common and hard to prevent even with great precautions, because one can be fooled so easily by the brightness or dullness of the sun on snow. All this I stored away in my budget of memories as I shall put on canvas someday the story of how terrible it is to be snow blind even though the condition may not last many days. It is not only terrifying, it is very painful!

We kept paddling until pretty late – until 9:30. At about eight o'clock the sun set and twilight lasted about an hour more. By that time, the moon came up and I noticed how strikingly beautiful the moonlight was, shining on the canoe paddle blades.

We were tiring, however, and soon decided to land on a small island in McKay Lake. This island had been the winter home of some trappers – about five teepees' worth! We pitched our tent, and when they found them, the men brought in some dead boughs which made a good bed. We turned in about 11:30, all three of us under one blanket, tent flaps open and a big fire going all night.

June 6, 1911. As there was a fairly strong and favorable wind blowing in the early morning, we started out with the sail up and were soon going faster than we could have paddled, but the wind got too heavy and we had to take down the sail. The waves were so high on the lake that we started to ship water and we were all rather frightened – not for ourselves, but for our precious cargo! The wind increased to a gale, and even though Fred certainly proved himself a prince of a canoe handler, it simply got too dangerous and at a little after nine o'clock we put in on the lee point of an island and all of us slept until two o'clock – dead tired.

Around two o'clock the wind died down and we left, made the end of McKay Lake, and turned into a small bay. As we enjoyed

Group of Indians in Eastern Ontario; 1911.
Lantern slide by F. E. Schoonover.

spite of our loads and the swampy footing. I carried 50 pounds by trump line just like the men – and also my camera. Part way, we met three *Nitchies*, but the unbelievable torment of the flies precluded any sociability and we passed with hardly a word. Before making a necessary second trip across the portage, we had supper on the Gaining Ground River where we put in at 9:30 in the evening to escape the flies.

We paddled in the moonlight until 1:15 in the morning, making the French post on Long Lake. Across the lake we could see a faint light which Fred told me was the Hudson's Bay Post, but we were too tired to risk going further. Just before we stopped, however, we crossed an Indian net. I went over it by the moonlight and removed three fine pike and one perch. Then we made a fire on a point the relief of smooth water, Fred told me of an Indian who had walked (snowshoed) 30 miles in four-and-a-half hours. He had been told by another that "Brown's horses drowned". But the man telling the story forgot the word for horses, so the message came out as "Brown drowned." On account of that, the Indian made the journey of 30 miles to the Post in the time stated, although I reflected that he must have had a powerful tail wind going for him!

Rounding a little bend in the bay, we came upon an Indian grave where we stopped for a minute or two. It was surrounded by a primitive hand-made fence. The tops of the corner posts were blue in color. On one cross hung a rosary; on the crosses of the graves of other Indians, balm of Gilead was hanging for remembrance. Rows of stones surrounded all the graves. For the men, it appeared simply a welcome rest, but for me it was another future picture. The men could not understand why I got so much more rest from this stop than they did!

At the end of the bay, which was actually the end of McKay Lake, we found a *Nitchie* Indian camp where there were only women. All the men had gone to the Post at Long Lake. I found myself again puzzled by the Indian reaction (if reaction it could be called), for they didn't pay the slightest attention to the fact that three strange men had entered their midst and that this might have been of consequence. I took a few photographs and we were off.

At this point we had reached the Height of Land. Actually this was a sort of savannah, called a muskeg. The Indians call it a "mashkig". In any event it was frightful. Clouds of black flies darkened the area and nothing, it seemed to us, could keep them off any exposed part of our bodies or our clothing. We found, of course, that our only hope of preserving our sanity was to keep moving as fast as we could. We made the two miles across in 30 minutes in

Portrait of an Innuit woman; 1911.
Lantern slide by F. E. Schoonover.

and laid out without even putting up the tent, pulling up an old Hudson's Bay Company boat as a windbreak.

Some *Nitchies* coming across Long Lake woke me up early, and we were all up by eight o'clock. I took some photographs of an old Indian and a squaw who passed the point in their birch bark canoe.

A half-breed, Joe Lavecque, and his Ojibwa wife landed at the point because his canoe was leaking. Joe said he was on his way to Jackfish, taking down mail, so while he was fixing his leak, I wrote a quick letter to my wife and turned it over with other mail to this North Country postman! Joe asked us to have some tea, and we accepted. But as Joe had none, we loaded our stuff in the canoe and paddled a short distance to the French post where the factor, a Mr. Spence, proved very hospitable and asked us to breakfast, one of canned meat, real bread and canned peaches!

After breakfast, we went across the lake, a trip of about a mile, to the Hudson's Bay Company Post where we met the factor, a Mr. Brown, to whom I explained our mission and desire to remain for a while. He couldn't have been more cordial, and his help and hospitality throughout our stay was interested and sincere. I could not have asked for better treatment.

The day of our arrival was well-timed and very rewarding after our hard work to get to the Post as quickly as we could. A fine brigade of four canoes came in about the middle of the day. These trappers and hunters had been out since January and February, and their evident pride in a good hunt was very evident. I got some fine photographs and had my sketching materials busy all day. Not in a long time had I had such a wealth of subject matter to work with. It was very thrilling. The men, too, seemed to be very happy – what little I saw of them. They were home!

June 8, 1911. This was the red-letter day! About the middle of the morning, the chief of the tribe and nine canoes came into sight. I was the first to greet him – Ogina (chief) Newatchegejickwabe. As he had neared the shore, he rose solemnly in the bow of the lead canoe, his bronze face lifted to the proud scrutiny of his friends. They landed on the point beyond the little church. As he debarked, no word was spoken as he grasped the hand of each in turn. I took many photographs, and saw an old powder horn and cloth gun cover that I could use for my costume collection!

The canoes were unloaded by the Indian women who then prepared a dinner, which in the North Country is at about eleven o'clock in the morning, of delicious lake trout for everyone who would partake. It was a magnificent occasion after which all went to the Company store to watch the Indians trade in their spring catch. It was no hit-and-miss affair! The protocol, though perhaps primitive to the uninitiated, was precise and great dignity was displayed. The Chief and honored members of his hunting party came first. Other hunters who had returned previously stepped out of the crowd surrounding the path of the fur-laden heroes and gave the solemn handshake.

The Chief was the first to hand in his skins – about $250 in all, all he could get for his entire hunt for the long, long spring. His hunt for the entire year would amount to but little over $400. He had many "rats" (muskrats), almost 100, plus mink valued at from $3 to $5 and a few fine otter at $25. The Chief also had the hunt of his daughter – rats only!

One member of the Chief's party who had had a debt of $600, and who had been blacklisted, produced a good hunt, bringing his debt to the Company down to $12. This reduction was not accomplished by just this year's hunt, however, but by it and those of two or three years back.

What amazed me was that some of the hunters seemed absolutely indifferent to the factor and his assessments as he went over the catch. It was not so much that they didn't understand, but that they seemed to have beautifully implicit faith in the factor. All stayed until the catches were completely turned in. My, what a picture this will make!

At the conclusion of the accounting for the catches, the Chief asked for his hat. With a display of superb showmanship, the factor turned around and carefully lifted it from a shelf where all had been admiring it. The factor came from behind the counter of furs with the bearing of a king and faced the Chief. Gently removing the Chief's old hat and handing it to him, he then placed the new hat, with CHIEF handsomely embroidered across the front, on the Chief's magnificent head.

June 9, 1911. Everyone was at the wharf this morning when we left the Post at 10:15, crossing Long Lake to put in on the Kagagami or English River. The first eight miles were smooth water, but then came a falls where we stopped for dinner. I put my fishing pole together and caught a two-and-a-half-pound trout which we cooked immediately. Some fire rangers passed as we were eating and warned us to be careful ahead. After they had gone, Fred told me not to worry as he knew every inch of the way in any direction we would be taking. "You take the fish," he said. "I take the canoe!" Right after lunch Fred shot us through the (two) bad rapids which the fire wardens must have had in mind, and it was beautiful to watch him handle the canoe, but there was no chance for me to show him that I could put on a little act too – with my fishing pole! The second rapids ended in another falls – beautiful, of course, as are all the many waterfalls in this area, but this meant another portage – one to the right and then a long one of a mile to the left. The flies were bad as we passed several winter camps, finally making camp ourselves near Pine Lake. We had to make a smudge in the tent, but got little sleep or rest and were up at four, making Pine Lake at about 5:30. Pine Lake was very beautiful. It was a little misty, but the little islands in the lake were very picturesque in the mist.

The whole scene was enlivened by the jumping of a great number of trout. Consequently, I put my rod together, and used all kinds of flies and spoons (mostly to entertain Fred!) and was delighted to find myself in the right spot at the very right time. I caught many spectacular trout, a number of which I threw back because we had no way to keep fresh food, and the fishing was so universally productive we had no worries about eating in the days ahead. We stopped at about ten o'clock at the lake outlet to eat and rest. On the way to the shore, I happened to see some pickerel feeding in the shallows, so while the men were preparing dinner, I took the canoe back out, put on a spoon and soon landed two big pike and a very long pickerel. I had three more big fish on, but they either got away by throwing out the lure or in one case by a mighty thrust that left me with only my pole and a snapped line. That kind of fishing was what I had come a long way to experience, and as I enjoyed it, I kept wondering if it really might be that I was the first white man to fish these choice waters!

Pine Lake can be described as a swelling of the English River. In the afternoon we had a very hard portage on the river. There were alternate stretches of swamp and waterfall, and the portages were very hard to find. I was now packing over 75 pounds. It was hot, and I was wringing wet from the exertion of the pack and the battle with the flies. In a short time I was terribly bitten, as human perspiration attracts these devilish biters.

Reaching a rapids which we thought would bring relief, Fred, in fact, told me that this rapids was safer to portage than to shoot. I could not bear the thought of another fly-clouded portage, however, and we decided to risk the water. Risk it was. This was a terrific rapids. Even with Fred's great skill with the paddle, we were shipping water and the blankets got wet. We missed the portage (just ahead of a bad falls) because of the very swift water. Heading for the falls, we bent our paddles for the shore. Luckily John grabbed a branch

Breakfast on the trail; 1911.
Lantern slide by F. E. Schoonover.

and I snatched one too so we were able to stop, but we had to work the canoe back through the swift rapids. Fred got in the water and pulled the canoe by tump line, as John and I poled with our paddles in a killing effort which finally brought us back to the portage we had missed. Here we had a discussion, as we were in poor shape and the portage was marked on our rough map as "Long Portage". Fred was not sure I should try it, although up to this point he had not shown the slightest indication that he did not have great confidence in my performance. I had been taking this as quite a compliment – coming from one of the best men on the water!

I was sorry later that I let my false pride overcome his suggestion that we stop and reorganize. However, I had been informed that at the end of this portage was the F.C.R. Construction Camp, where it might be more advantageous to "regroup and recover".

We could not make this miserable portage in one trip, because the wet things were too heavy. Fred went ahead with the canoe and John and I followed, only to find that at the end of the portage the F.C.R. people must have moved farther on. Very disappointed, we left what we had brought and decided to return immediately for the rest of our gear. This was disastrous. We lost our way as it began to rain heavily. We must have made many circles looking for high ground to get our bearing. Luckily, it cleared and we found a point of rock. We built a fire and decided to remain the night. Like the cloud with the silver lining, the night provided the greatest display of northern lights I had ever seen.

At four o'clock the next morning Fred roused us to say that he could get us back on the portage now which somehow he did, and we went back over it to the river. Here we made some breakfast, but under what must have been the worst conditions yet. Murphy had to keep skimming the flies and mosquitoes off the tea, but the tea revived us a bit, and after distributing the load evenly between ourselves we put the long portage behind us for the second time – a very hard walk over windfalls and through muskegs so dense with mosquitoes that the creatures seemed to have nowhere to light but on us!

Our gear was a mess, but we put it in the canoe and headed into the rapids. They were pretty bad – absolutely the worst I had ever been in. We shipped the canoe at least a third full of water going through and were all very nervous. Even Fred was nervous, for he could not control the canoe with so much water in it and we could not stop until we found an eddy at the end of the swift, rocky stretch.

Although we did not know it at the time, we were not much

more than around a bend away from the construction camp haven! We had to stop, not knowing that so little distance separated us from our planned stop. We pulled ashore, got the water out of the canoe and reloaded everything. After a fresh start we reached the camp in a few minutes!

The men couldn't have been more wonderful. Because it was Sunday, they were not working and all pitched in to help us get dried out. We were made very much at home. It started raining about noon, however, so all of us spent all afternoon sleeping. Because it continued to rain all that day our gear stayed wet, and we could not move out. Fortunately, it cleared the next day, but it took us all day to get our gear in any shape to travel.

June 13, 1911. We left the construction camp at seven, a bright and early hour considering all we had been through. During the morning we made several short and one long portage. In the middle of the afternoon we made a very exciting drop over a falls. Although the direct drop was only three feet, we hit it at an angle. Old Mother Nature has no trouble fooling even such a master of the canoe as Fred. We all thought it was over for us, but in some manner we got through.

How quickly one recovers from such fright, I thought, as a little later in the afternoon I was out by myself in a quiet eddy catching our evening meal of trout. From frightful terror to the equally exciting pleasure of fishing made a tremendous impression on me. Now I feel I can get these experiences which I have been describing down on canvas with the spirit I have wanted so much to have in my painting of the great Canadian North Country!

June 14, 1911. All of us were up and moving around at 4:30. Not wanting to hold up the men, I managed to have a superb trout breakfast in less than half an hour. My, what fishing! They bite as though they had never seen food, yet the pair of beauties I brought in must have spent their lives eating.

This was to be our last day going downstream. Inasmuch as we had long since traversed the height of land, the water was flowing almost due north toward Hudson Bay, or toward the North Pole as we liked to think of it! We left camp at six o'clock for our northernmost stop, the Hudson's Bay Company Post at Mammamattawa. At the end of the first two hours' paddling, we rested for ten minutes, but we still made 25 miles by 11 o'clock when, as is the North Country custom, we stopped for dinner. Fortunately there was a

Exterior of Hudson's Bay Company Post, Mammamattawa, Ontario; 1911.
Lantern slide by F. E. Schoonover.

Interior of Hudson's Bay Company Post, 1911.
Lantern slide by F. E. Schoonover.

strong head wind blowing and not many flies and mosquitoes bothered us. It was nice not to have to skim them off the tea for a change! In spite of the strong head wind we made the Post by four-thirty, aided by a strong current and several rapids. As I figure it, we have made almost 50 miles today.

At the Post about 15 Indians were waiting on the bank to watch and welcome us. The factor himself was an Indian and spoke good English, but though his welcome was warm and sincere, we found this Post is a barren, desolate, and foresaken place! Nevertheless, we were glad to arrive, and the genuine show of hospitality we received in great part made up for the unfortunate nature of the location. We put up our tent near the factor's house, but the bugs were so bad that we could not go into the bush to get boughs for a bed. I don't know how these people ever get used to the bugs. If we had not had our bug protectors in the tent, I don't think we could have slept with just the smudge. Before retiring we purchased one can of preserved meat, some hardtack and a supply of matches at the Post store. The factor asked me if we had heard of any great sickness along the way. I didn't realize at first that this would really be the only kind of news that would provide the kind of information they could understand or even be concerned with. He seemed very happy that we do not bring sickness or news of it!

Although I was very tired, I used all the light that remained to make sketches. I had already taken a chance on the light that accompanied our arrival to take a few photos, especially of the group gathered to welcome us.

June 15, 1911. We were all up before the Indians, but before we had finished packing the canoe, the factor came out and said goodbye and wished us a safe trip home. As we passed the high, clay bank, the whole village was out. They made no sign.

The Nagagami River was very high and swift. Consequently we had the hardest day of the trip – terribly hard – paddling against the rapids all day. During the afternoon we rested every five minutes. Usually we had rested only five minutes every hour! We had endeavored to make the first portage, but as the paddling was so hard, we stopped short of the portage on the left bank of the river near a very sweet spring.

June 16, 1911. During the night the water had receded eight inches! Shortly after leaving – about one hour's travel – we made the first portage. The water still was sufficiently high that we did not have to land and go to all the trouble of a carry and a battle with the bugs.

As a matter of fact, the pull turned out not to be too hard as the right bank of the river was gravel. I harnessed to the trump line and pulled the canoe while John paddled in the bow and Fred poled in the stern. We passed two Indian camping grounds which appeared to be at least three or four years old.

The portage was not too time-consuming, and I enjoyed the variety it offered. We were now well used to hard work, and I guess in pretty good physical condition. As my part of the pull kept me in the cool water, I rather congratulated myself on having chosen what is usually the most demanding job in this particular manoeuver!

It was not long before we were all back in the canoe again. Shortly after, we met a party of two big canoes and three small ones, all coming down the River Nagagami. We made shore together. The large party of voyagers was headed by a Mr. Tempents of the Algoma Central and Hudson Bay Railway which joins the Canadian National at Hearst in the Cochrane district. His party was headed for Hudson Bay. With him were some Cree Indians and a hunter by the name of Linkielle, who told me that at the last of the three portages ahead there was an outcropping of gold quartz. He had taken a sample that (and this in great confidence and in a whisper) had traces of gold in it!

Tempents' party had lost one Indian in the Kabinakagami River while running a rapids. After that the Indians refused to continue on the Kabinakagami so the party had portaged to the White River, an awkward effort.

While we stood about talking, the large party cooked dinner, but we were not asked to join. After they left, we continued. A couple of miles further up we stopped and had our cup of tea.

We were hard put to find a good camping place that night. We kept going until it was almost dark, finally stopping at the river edge on the left bank. It was a very poor place, but we had had a long day and were so tired that we only bothered to put up the fly canopy. This did not work very well, so about ten o'clock we had to put up the tent. There were so many mosquitoes that nothing worked against them and no one slept. It was a hard night.

June 17, 1911. In one hour-and-a-half we made three portages, pulling over one and making two carries. At the end of the last we came to the place from which I thought Linkielle had taken his gold quartz sample. Just for the heck of it, we did some prospecting. We did not get rich on Linkielle's nonsense, but the foolishness put us in good spirits for dinner there. I had a lot of fun kidding with the men about

Rapids on the Kenogami; 1911.
Lantern slide by F. E. Schoonover.

the wealth we were sitting on while drinking our tea and eating our beans!

It was lucky we had had some fun, because the afternoon was one of very hard pulling and poling. We made camp near a deserted Indian wigwam, the poles of which we tore down for firewood. We may not have found gold, but we made up for that with the easy firewood – much more realistic! Still in good spirits we made an excellent camp and celebrated by shaving – the first time in about a week!

June 18, 1911. This proved to be the hardest day of all on the water. We were from six to 10:30 doing four-and-a-half miles, mostly accomplished by cutting trail along the river bank and pulling the canoe by trump line. We had been working to reach Highwood Portage, pulling through some hellish rapids. We were all getting tired, but locating the portage and the chance to make this particular circumvention gave us a "second wind." High Portage is indeed properly named. The three-mile trip is right over a mountain, and I was packing 50 pounds. At the end, however, we found a camp of engineers and had a fine Sunday dinner with them. Afterwards we went back over the portage to get the rest of our stuff. On the return trip, I packed 100 pounds, the heaviest load I have tried.

Today was a beautiful sunny day, a fact that was terribly important to us because our blankets and much of our clothing had not been dry in a number of days – actually not since going down the river to the Indian post. The engineers helped us rig a drying arrangement and while we were making the second trip over High Portage our things dried out pretty well, but it was hot and carrying the heavy loads over the mountain made us soaking wet. We decided to do some washing (again with the help of the engineers to whom I was able to make a promise of fresh fish, for while they were working the next morning I decided to fish while the last of the drying was completed). Never have I experienced such fishing!

Even though I missed the early part of the day, which is best for fishing, I found my wet flies very effective. To vary my program, I started out with a Parmachenie Belle (which proved effective enough), but I switched to a Silver Doctor after landing three enormous brook trout in a very short time. The Silver Doctor also enticed these Northern brook fellows, who seemed to have no apparent choice of taste. After boating another couple of beauties I put on a Jack Scott #7 and later a Brown Palmer Peacock #7. Both these worked well, too.

The water was running slowly and I was able to concentrate

on my fishing rather than on manoeuvering the canoe. After a while, however, I happened upon a spot where a small stream emptied into the river, and knowing the habits of the trout, I dropped a small stone anchor so that I stayed just above the confluence. In the half hour I stayed, I landed 16 fine brook trout. It was wonderful sport and I had no feeling of guilt over taking so many with those hungry engineers waiting to see if my boasting would amount to anything!

All good things have to come to an end, and this magnificent morning was no exception, but I was a happy man when I eased my big catch into camp. Even the hardest of the men could not restrain his amazement, and we had the biggest dinner and supper of the trip. I had a hard time believing this luck myself, particularly the fact that all the fish were big brook trout!

Over the next few days, I scheduled time for fishing. The trout were running up-river like salmon. I seemed to land the biggest with a Jack Scott #7, and on my last outing on the river before entering Lake Nagagami, I ran into trout so big I began to lose them. I lost six in a row while Fred watched much amused – as though it served me right to be toned down a bit. The sixth one broke the tip of my rod, and Fred said he thought that one would have weighed well over four pounds, but we already had a couple of four-pounders in the canoe and so I was still quite happy, particularly about the fact that I always carry an extra end section for my pole. It will have to last me from here to the end of the trip, as there was, we found, no way to repair the broken one.

June 23, 1911. We finished with the Nagagami River today. At this end where it sources from Nagagami Lake, there are not many rapids and the going was not bad – not when compared with the part between Mammamattawa Post and High Wood Portage! Nagagami Lake is not large and we crossed it easily and quickly, as there was a good breeze blowing from the north and we raised our red silk sail again.

At the beginning of Obakamiga Lake, which is not too far from Nagagami Lake, we stopped for dinner on the first of two small islands. Navigating this lake was very hard as it was cut up into many small bays. In fact, we had quite a bit of trouble finding the outlet, going into three small bays without result before we found the right one. After leaving the larger part of the lake, we passed through a long, winding, beautiful stretch of dead water. The banks were lined with spruce and birch, and the edge of the water was fringed with water lillies. We saw several winter and summer camps with moose horns, bird wings, and bits of ribbon hanging on the bush in various places. There were poles in the water for Indian nets and also racks for the drying of fish.

At the end of the narrow channel I saw fish jumping, so as soon as the place was marked for our camp, I took the duffel out of the canoe, put my rod together, and went back to the place where I had seen the fish. I first tried my favorite Jack Scott #7 and then a Cow Dung without too much success, although success was getting to be a relative term. But I hooked a wall-eyed pike on a Scarlet Ibes. They seemed to bite very freely, so I experimented adding a spoon. This proved a good idea. As a matter of fact with the run being on on all of the big fish, almost anything I tried on them worked. It was really no test of skill. In all I caught about 30 large fish, out of which I saved eight of the best. I could have continued the catch, but I was getting hungry myself and I knew the men certainly were.

I was sad when I waved goodbye to this experience, because I knew this would be our last night together on this expedition.

The spot for the camp was beautiful, overlooking the lake, and after John had prepared a grand supper which we ate with great relish, I watched the lake become moonlit and dreamed of how I would put it all on canvas – an Indian in a bark canoe, clear in the full brightness of the moon, in great and noble primitive majesty. Finally I could see the picture, actually see it, and I know I will paint it exactly as I caught it this night!

But this was not our last night! I turned in after the men had fallen asleep. For the first time the mosquito net did not have to be put up, as it was very cold and there did not seem to be many flies about.

June 24, 1911. It had been a very cold night, and I had wrapped up my head as well as my body. We were up at 4:20, and breakfast was over and we had started at 5:20, determined to make the Canadian Pacific Railway in time to have the late afternoon train pick us up. But as I noted above, we had not had our last camping night, and today we did not make the railway.

The day started well, and we reached the end of Obokamiga Lake, paddling at four to five miles an hour. There we took the Height of Land Portage which is about a mile long and then made the successful passage of several small lakes to Gum River. As we entered it, we noticed some driftwood floating along with us, and we were and should have been apprehensive. By the time we reached the first rapids, we found the river now full of drifting wood. But we could not stop as there was no shore! In this first rapids, we had

As Darkness Closed over the North Country; 1921.
Oil; 40 x 28.

our most narrow escape of the trip. Except for John's magnificent work at the bow, the canoe might have been ripped to ribbons. As it was, we suffered bad damage and were awfully lucky to get through to where the Gum quiets. Here we had to stop for repairs and for the night; but what did turn out to be our last night in camp was a happy one, for we were alive, and there were many times that day when we did not think we would be!

Shaken, but triumphant, we did make the Canadian Pacific line the next day and flagged the evening train. We loaded our gear, including the canoe, into the baggage car, and I was on my way to Toronto. John and Fred got off at White River after a short ride. Fred wrote me later that the next day they rode back to Jackfish so they, not I, really made the round trip!

Frank Schoonover's Canadian experiences were to stay in his mind in epic clarity for more than 70 beautifully productive years!

Red Blanket Sail; 1927.
Oil; 32 x 42.

Fishing in the North Country; 1912.
Oil; 24 x 34.

Pickerel; 1917.
Oil; 24 x 34.

The Portage; 1927.
Oil; 16 x 34.

Indians coming ashore at Long Lake, Ontario; 1911.
Lantern slide and hand tinting by F. E. Schoonover.

The Trailmakers; 1941.
Oil; 42 x 29.

The Spirit of the Wendigo; 1968.
Oil; 20 x 16.

Part Three

The
Canadian
Stories

The inspiration for all of Schoonover's writings stemmed from his adventures in the Canadian North. His day books represent the raw material, while the magazine articles which were published between 1905 and 1921 are the refined culmination of his experiences. These articles, plus the illustrations he created to accompany them, communicate the essence of the spirited Canadian frontier and its people.

The first story to come from Schoonover's Canadian experience appeared in the April, 1905 issue of Scribner's Magazine, and bore the intriguing title, "The Edge of the Wilderness". It is the artist's personal account of his daring travel in the bitter Canadian winter and ends with his departure into the wilderness, away from all civilization. His winter adventures are continued in the story "Breaking Trail" which appeared in a later issue of Scribner's Magazine.

"The Fur-Harvesters" portrays some vivid scenes from his summer journey. Much detail is given in this article to the people who inhabit the North.

Schoonover wrote a general sketch of his travels in the article "Bringing the Outdoors In", addressing himself to the young would-be adventurers who read The American Boy magazine. This article also gives insight into Schoonover's attitude towards his craft as an artist.

The short story "The Snow Baby" is a lovely piece of fiction which depicts a more gentle side of the North.

Schoonover's tales of adventure are faithful Canadiana, factually accurate, and characterized by his special attunement to the vivid and virile wilderness of the Canadian North. They are based on actual experiences and best speak for themselves.

The Edge of the Wilderness

At the Threshold

Upon an evening early in January, the bitterest time of the mid-winter season, I found myself in the snow-buried Canadian wilderness, upon the borderland of civilization. The twilight was fading as we approached the Indian Reserve at Pointe Bleue. The sleigh-bells rang out thin and clear in the deadly cold, sounding as though from a great distance away. The Canadian sleigh or cariole was red against the white, its low body resting on broad runners that terminated in great iron-shod curves that cut sharply through the deep snow. We had been riding all afternoon against the cruel north wind, blowing a temperature of forty-five degrees below zero across a barren level and a lake thirty miles wide. Wrapped warmly in a raccoon-skin coat and cap with my body turned sideways to the icy cutting of the wind, I had been watching the fast fading of the Northern day. The few thin trees were black against the yellow gray of the sky, and now the pink of the snow was fast dissolving into the deeper purple of the coming night. Now and then, while the daylight was still bright, I had caught from the tops of the little hillocks an occasional glimpse of the far-distant village; its gaily painted houses – red, yellow, and green – were gaudy against the snow; the clustering flag-poles, each topped with some symbol – an Indian, a beaver, a fish, or the like – were bright against the sky. Now all had turned gray in the coming twilight save for one touch of golden yellow on high where the big cross of the church caught the sinking sun and turned to flame. Then that flame also faded out, even as I watched, and suddenly everything seemed very desolate.

Then there were signs of life. The snow, which had blown a level expanse across the road, was broken once by a snow-shoe track. On the frozen lake an Indian boy was filling a pail with water at the waterhole. In front of a log cabin, protected on the north side by great strips of birch bark, some dogs were howling for admittance from the bitter twilight cold. Pressed against the one clear glass of a heavily frosted window, I saw a dark face watching us as we passed. Then my mood changed again and I felt a sudden thrill of pleasure as I realized that here at least I was indeed upon the threshold of that

First published in *Scribner's Magazine*, April 1905.

strange frozen wilderness I had come so far to see.

Winding about the edge of the wind-swept lake, we passed the rapidly darkening houses of the village and so came to the store of the Hudson's Bay Company and the home of the factor. Then I rapped at the kitchen door (for the others were blocked with huge snow-drifts), and a French Canadian opened it and took me through an outer shed into the kitchen beyond. My journey was done! How comfortable and warm it felt to be again in a human habitation after that long, long stretch of snowy wilderness and the long, long hours of lonely arctic travel.

I was three days in this outpost of civilization, where the wild life of the north and the tamer life I had left behind me met and joined hands. It was very strange and new to me, and very pregnant of that existence I was to see lying beyond.

During this time I lodged in the house of an independent or free trader. He was rough as the north woods makes a man rough, and I remember he drove his bargain for board and lodging with me at the house door before I was permitted to enter.

My first taste of the borderland life is very distinct in my budget of memories. The family, I remember, were all in the kitchen when I entered. They rose and stood and stared at me. The supper was on the table, and my appetite was sharp after the long day's travel in the cariole. So I sat down with right good-will upon the long wooden bench with the free trader and his four sons, and ate the cold fat pork and the hot meat-pie with ravenous satisfaction.

Afterward I pulled a heavy chair close to the three-decker wood-stove (which stands in nearly every such Canadian house in the cut partition between the bedroom and the kitchen) and watched the smoke from the many pipes drift about the room, obscuring a large wooden cross and colored print of the Bleeding Heart above the door. From the room it was drawn, a thin blue film, through an opening in the wooden ceiling and into the sleeping room above.

So it was all very strange and wonderful to my foreign eyes – this far-away frontier life of civilization into which I had come.

With the factor's help I secured good guides – hunters who would have shortly gone to their trapping-grounds, but who, on the assurance of good pay, were willing to undertake the long journey with me. The older of the two men was a full-blooded Montagnais Indian, by name Xavier Gill; a man of great endurance, broad-shouldered, lean-flanked, and thin-legged. His face was very dark, like a bronze; his hair hung straight and glossy black over the high cheek-bones, and the small bead-like eyes gleamed like two bits of fire. A silent man was he, but one able to cope with any emergency, as I found later.

The other guide, and the younger, was a Scotchman – the son of the factor at Abitibi. From his continual living with the Indians and from his Indian wife he had gathered a knowledge of the language of the Tadabull and Montagnais. With him for an interpreter, and with some Canadian *patois*, I contrived to understand and to make myself understood by the Indians whom I afterward met.

From Gill I procured two dogs – one his own, one from his Indian father-in-law. Each of the men had his own sleigh, and a third was made for the two dogs.

These sleighs are low, narrow, and about five feet long. The sides, shod with iron runners, are held together by seven or eight wooden rungs. Stout pieces of twine fastened to these hold the loads of one hundred and fifty to two hundred pounds.

In the matter of provisions and camp necessaries, I followed the Indians' advice absolutely. Our supplies included tea, flour, salt pork, lard and beans; some pepper, salt, a little baking-powder (white and maple) – just to "start us," as the trappers say. Two or three tin pails, four tin dishes and cups, a spoon or two, and the frying-pan completed the outfit. The men each had a white blanket – the "four-point" size of the Hudson's Bay Company. My own were made of a coarse woollen cloth or duffel, the post's supply of blankets being "traded out". I bought eight yards, four of which I made into a kind of sleeping-bag, and the remainder, without cutting, served as a double blanket.

It was quite dark and a lamp had to be lighted before all our supplies had been gone over a second time and packed in dunnage bags, ready for the morning's start.

"Everything is all right, Xavier?" I asked.

"Yes, m'sieur."

"Enough provisions?"

"Yes."

And so we were ready for the wilderness.

In the morning, the supplies were packed in two carioles, and with the three small sleighs trailing and the two dogs running free, we left behind us our last civilized resting-place and turned our faces toward the Northern wilds. It was nine o'clock in the morning and early daylight.

At noon the following day the supplies were dumped on the snow, sleighs loosed, and the carter, with a *bon voyage*, turned his great, long wood-sleigh about and left us.

The Wilderness Folk

The evening of the second day from the post we emerged from the bush through which the trail had led, and stopped upon the edge of a lake to rest the dogs, for the pulling had been hard and the loads were heavy. As I stood there, I saw, far cross, at the end of the lake, a thin blue smoke arising and I heard the sounds of barking dogs. It was my first Indian village that lay there brooding in the profound snow of the wilderness.

As we approached across the lake, following a recently made trail, two Indian girls suddenly appeared from the fringe of dark green spruce bush and approached us. Perhaps they thought we were returning friends, for as we drew near, they stopped, watched us intently a moment, and then suddenly turned and hurried away up the snowy hill and were lost to view in great clouds of snow churned up by the snow-shoes that clapped and flapped like the wings of huge clumsy birds.

Then there was the first real sign of their home life – the water-hole cut in the ice, and beside it a homely well-worn axe, its blade heavy with accumulated layers of thin ice. A tall spruce bough marked the opening, to save the cutting of a new hole after each drifting storm.

Up the steep ascent, we pulled the loads, past the bordering fringe of white birch, past the tracks of many snow-shoes, through the thin curtain of the green balsam and spruce, and in an instant we were in the midst of an Indian village.

Darkness was beginning to fall, and against the gloomy spruce bush behind the five tent huts cut sharply – spots of yellow and brown against the dark background of foliage. Many toboggans, long and narrow with delicately curved bows, were leaning against the surrounding trees. Snow-shoes, small and great, were to be seen everywhere hung upon the branches or stuck in the snow near the tents. Some blankets were hanging upon a frame ghostly white in the gathering dark.

From the tents the Indians stared at us. Their eyes glistened brightly as they stolidly watched us – strange wayfarers in their lonely frozen haunt – pass like spirits in the gloaming through their village. All about us was a bedlam of snarling and barking dogs, but no one came forth but two little boys who accompanied us up the snowy rise, upon the other side of which we were to make our camp for the night.

Just as I reached the top of the hill, I stopped and looked back. The entire village, young and old, had now gathered in a crowd

Top:
One of the two Indian Boys who
helped us up the Hill; 1904.
*Mechanical reproduction of
pastel drawing; 8 x 8.*

Bottom left:
Photograph from which the
drawing was executed.

Bottom right:
The other Indian Boy, Son of
Tommo Awa-Sheesh; 1904.
Pastel drawing; 9½ x 7.

against the twilight gray of the snow, staring after the strange visitors who had thus come unbidden and unheralded into their wonderful world of stillness and whiteness.

We dwelt five days in this strange world, which had been so remote in my studio, and of which I was now a living part. In those five days I came to know all the people, from the chief to the little baby wrapped in its swaddling clothes of moss and bark. I haunted their tents so that I brought home their life in my traps when I returned to civilization.

The village was only a temporary one. Here some Cree, Montagnais, and some Indians from the St. Maurice had been living for three or four weeks. It was the time of the New Year's season, when many of the trappers pack the skins of the fall hunt upon toboggans, journey to the post, make a trade, and return with provisions for the spring hunt. This happened to be a common meeting-place, and here for a few weeks the men lingered to smoke and talk and the women to make snow-shoes and the children to set snares for the rabbits. From here the various trails would separate, leading them far apart, black specks in that desolate, unknown Northland.

Down the hill I went next morning with my camera, sketching pad, and colored chalks toward the village. Back of the tents four or five of the children were coasting down the hill on one of the long, narrow toboggans – evidently an old one given to them, for the color had long since changed from the brilliant yellow to a silvery gray and the bow was patched with a strip of birch bark and lashed about many times with strings of caribou. Seeing me with my strange instrument, they stopped their sport and followed me into the camp. I had some mint candies in my pocket, and I gave them each a few; after that we were the best of friends.

Two Indian women, their black hair gathered under red handkerchiefs, were chopping wood, but upon my approach they immediately went into their tents. Outside the tent, the one nearest the lake, an Indian was packing provisions on a dog-sleigh for a short journey. He was small and very dark – a man about forty. As I and my guides came up he straightened himself and nodded to us. Xavier approached him and asked about a toboggan.

"Yes," he said, "there was a woman camping just a little journey over the hill – so" – he pointed with the stem of his pipe – "and she had just made a toboggan."

"And would she sell it?"

"Yes, she might sell it; it was a chance."

So Xavier left and I spoke to the Indian again through my other guide.

"Ask him, Skene," I asked, "if I can go into his tent and make a drawing."

Skene had to explain very carefully just what I wanted, for the Indian could not understand why one should come so far for such a strange purpose. It was only the traders and an occasional Government surveyor who would venture thus in the bitter cold.

"Well, Skene," I asked, "is it all right for me to go into the tent?"

"Yes, m'sieur."

"And you explained about the drawing?"

"Yes; the Indian says he's going off now for a two day's journey, but he will wait a little while if you want to draw a portrait of him."

As I entered the tent I had to step down quite two feet, for the snow had been packed, and the floor, spread deep with balsam boughs, was far below the usual level. They all stared at me as I stood inside the canvas walls. The family was large – the mother, a grown son and daughter, many children, and dogs without number. In the crowded tent home they made a place, the woman even providing me with a blanket. I sat down upon it and the floor of balsam boughs. That floor of boughs had at one time been clean and fresh from the trees, but was now dry and covered with the refuse of many days of living and eating and smoking.

The snow just inside the tent-wall had not been packed and upon this little shelf were the blankets, clothing, the provisions – all the personal belongings of the family. Upon little forked sticks hung the cups, the powder-horns, and the beads and crosses of the Church. Just within the door-opening, resting on four green birch posts, was the little sheet-iron stove. The canvas was protected from the red heat of the many-jointed stove-pipe by the rim of an old tin plate. About the stove were the dogs and the cooking utensils.

Such was the interior of an Indian's winter house as I first saw it, and those I came to know afterward were all of a like sort.

I passed my tobacco-pouch to Tommo Awa-sheesh, who gravely filled his black pipe and handed the tobacco to his wife. She in turn filled her pipe, and passed the pouch to daughter and son, and so it went from one to another until the entire family, except the baby, had filled their pipes and were smoking.

Then with Tommo's consent, I set about making a sketch. From the outside the Indians peeped into the tent, crowding about and watching me as I worked. Two little boys wriggled in from the black mass that filled the doorway, came over to where I was and sat down, one beside me, the other directly between Tommo and myself. When I finished the drawing, I presented the woman with the likeness of

Top:
Photograph from which the drawing
was executed.

Bottom:
A Bit of Domestic Life; 1904.
Crayon and pastel; 11 x 16.

her chief; she took it, looked at it, shrieked and laughed, and shrieked and shrieked again. They passed it back and forth, and finally handed it to Tommo, framed black with many greasy thumb marks. Tommo made no comment of any sort. He rolled the paper very carefully, tied it with a piece of red cloth, and put it with some treasures in an old flour-bag.

In this tent I also made sketches of the two little boys. One of them when I had finished took the yellow piece of chalk that I had given him as a reward, and with his back to the family, produced on a strip of birch bark a caribou with no horns, a very lean neck, and legs that would travel in either direction.

Thus I gained my first footing with my new friends.

The short January day was darkening as I laid aside my colors and looked upon that wild life, unchanged through generations of ancestors. I watched the Indian mother preparing a little bag of blankets and of moss for the baby. The baby was very fat and very dark, with black glossy hair and tiny black slits for eyes; it reminded me of a Japanese doll. Upon a little square of blankets, she spread a layer of soft green moss from the black spruce. Upon this she laid the little, squirming atomy. She drew the fur cap well down upon its head, and upon each foot she pulled a rabbit-skin sock with the fur inside. The blanket, the cloth, and the moss were all folded about the little one and laced together very tightly with strings of caribou hide. She laid the little pappoose into a hammock made by throwing a small red and green blanket across two ropes tied at either end to poles. Then she swung it back and forth, singing a high minor song of only a few notes' range. Doubtless this was the way a thousand years ago that the Indian baby was packed and swung and crooned to of a winter's night.

The following morning I endeavored to make a color drawing of this very thing, but somehow, the mother resented it. She became uneasy and left the tent. I found afterward she had hunted up Xavier Gill, my Indian, and asked if I intended any harm. Nor did Xavier's assurances satisfy her, and so I had to give over my purpose. I did not insist, for there were other tents I wished to visit, and the friendship of the Indians was well worth keeping. But with other families, I had no difficulty; they seemed quite willing for me to come and go as I pleased.

I became really intimate with the chief, a Cree Indian. His name was Pierre Kurtness, and he was a conjuror. He was possessed of all the legends, lore, and traditions of the woods handed down to him through a thousand generations of ancestors and only just hidden with a thin veneer of so-called Christianity. In his tent I was always welcome, and when I proposed to draw his likeness he seemed quite well pleased. I had only been working a few minutes when he stopped his "sitting' and hunted up a little scarlet bag embroidered with many-colored beads. From it he took a bundle of rags. This he un-rolled with great care, as if some treasure were hidden in the dirty wrappings, and I wondered what it could be. Then from the last fragments he produced a broken piece of comb and began soberly combing his hair.

I was at work a long while on this sketch and the old fellow got very uneasy toward the last; his legs became quite stiff from the continual kneeling, but he held the pose and would never admit he was tired. He was very proud of the drawing and held it up so those in the door-way could see it. Afterward I added, while he was watching, some dots with white chalk to the picture of the handkerchief about his neck. This seemed especialy wonderful and brought forth a long guttural "Ah!" I thanked him, gave him a plug of tobacco, and left the tent.

It was late in the afternoon and the light was fading. I entered a tent somewhat removed from the others — the only one I had not yet visited. At the end an Indian was seated. He made no comment of any sort save the customary "Good evening". He was quite alone, seated with his back to the canvas. I soon saw he was very sick. Like animals, his kind had left him to suffer alone; like an animal he brooded upon his sufferings in solitude as he waited for the disease to spend itself. I watched him; but he was quite indifferent to my gaze, and neither of us spoke. Gradually the darkness settled deeper and deeper. He became a hunched brown shape against the tent; his head sank deep between his shoulders and, from under the lids, his eyes burned with the fever of the disease. So I left him.

The sense of this dreadful thing affected me very profoundly and I felt a great relief as I carefully fastened the tent-flap and passed beyond into the stillness and pureness of the winter's night.

During the long night a soft snow had sifted over the camp, and when I looked out from the tent the sun was shining brightly upon a thousand little snow-pads that hung heavy upon the spruce and balsam. All about the tents, covering the accumulated filth of days, lay a pure new blanket, reflecting from millions of crystalline surfaces the yellow of the morning sun.

As it was a fine day for hunting, I sent the men off in the hopes that they might bag two or three "*uapush*" (rabbits) or a partridge, and so save the flour and pork. I watched them as they clattered off upon their snow-shoes across the lake and over the hills, the long fringes of the many-colored sash fluttering in the wind, and the powder-horns cutting a brilliant streak across their coats.

Pierre Kurtness; 1904.
Mechanical reproduction of crayon and pastel drawing; 12 x 18.

As I stood there the daughter of Tommo Awa-sheesh came swinging down the trail back of the tents, throwing up clouds of new white with every lift of her broad snow-shoes. She had been three or four miles that morning looking over her own traps – fifteen or twenty of them set for rabbits near the trail up the hill and along the frozen creek. Down the hill she came and across the solid swamp, a small tomahawk axe in her hand and some rabbits tied with birch twigs swinging from her shoulder. When quite near me she stopped and we looked at each other in silence. She was very picturesque. The round dark face with the black hair blowing across it, breathed forth the very soul of a healthful and vigorous life. The very poise of her body and the grip of her moccasins on the snow-shoes told of a continual battle for existence in that pitiless North. She wore about her neck a small flag – the English union-jack – and upon it hung a big metal cross. By way of making another friend I offered her a silk handkerchief. She stood and looked at it a long time. Then she suddenly snatched it from me and ran clattering away through the bush to her own camp.

At noon when my guides returned I told them what I had done. They laughed long and heartily. I did not then know, as I afterward found, what a serious interpretation the girl must have placed upon the offering. I believe I would never have been able to get my rabbit blanket excepting for the possessorship she thenceforth felt in me. The white man in the wilderness cannot be too careful as to how he conducts himself in such affairs.

These rabbit blankets, by the way, are made of the skins cut into strips and loosely woven into furry robes. They are very warm, and I used my own with great comfort wrapped about my shoulders every night as I slept through all that long semi-arctic journeying.

As the day approached for my departure, I went down into the village to pay a last visit to my strange friends. It was night, and the coldness of the air was very bitter in its intensity. One of the tents, lit from within, was brighter than the others. I could see the great black shadows, some sharp, others blurred, moving about on the candle-lit canvas walls, and as I passed I heard the sound of many voices within. I entered; the gayly colored circle of men, women, and children moved together, making a place for me, near the stove. They were playing a game of cards for little paper bundles of sulphur matches, seated about a white Hudson's Bay Company blanket. One candle fastened to a stick with a piece of birch bark, gave them light and threw those great shadows on the tent behind them. I have rarely seen a more picturesque sight than that group gathered in the dimly lighted tent – the women, with red and yellow handkerchiefs about their heads, green and blue waists and moccasins of all descriptions.

Maria Awa-Sheesh, Daughter of Tommo Awa-Sheesh; 1904.
Crayon; 18 x 11½.

A Cree Indian Woman; 1904.
Mechanical reproduction of crayon and pastel drawing; 12 x 18.

One of the girls was alternately smoking and playing a harmonica. Near the stove a little girl was making for herself a doll from a squirrel-skin. Far back in the shadows a boy wrapped in a rabbit-skin coat was trying to sleep. All about the sides of the tent were the blankets and the cooking utensils. Upon forked sticks hung a collection of tin cups, muzzle-loading guns, powder-horns, the bullet and cap pouch and high above these, just emerging from the big black shadows of their shoulders and heads, glittered the many crosses and beads of the Church. So I watched them as they played, winning and losing little packages, until they tired of the game and stopped.

Then I asked, through my guide, for directions to the camp of a trapper, one Semo Mac-nee-call, an Indian thought to be hunting about six day's journey from the camp. A St. Maurice Indian, kneeling near the candle-light, drew upon a Hudson's Bay Company bag a map of the trail. About him gathered all the inmates of the tent looking over one another's heads and shoulders, and each giving advice to the map-maker. With this paper-bag map I travelled for many days over an absolutely unbroken trail.

The next morning before the breaking of the day I left the still sleeping camp and turned my face toward the blank wilderness of white in which I was to dwell for so many days to come.

Breaking Trail

It was the early gray of the morning and the Indian village was still asleep. It seemed very strange to see it for the last time thus wrapped as it were, in a garment of silence. Before us lay the boundless white northern wilderness into which we proposed to break our trail.

First went Xavier Gill, who broke trail. His snowshoes clicked in the silence one against the other with each step that he took. Behind him trailed a long narrow toboggan, loaded with a hundred and fifty pounds of provisions. This he drew by a broad leather band called a trump-line or portage strap. This strap passes across the forehead (so that the hands may be free) and is attached to the bow of the toboggan. Next behind him followed Skene, and then came the dogs, each harnessed to a sledge, heavily loaded with two hundred pounds of provisions. Last of all came the author – the end of the long train that wound its serpent-like way through the breaking day and into the silence of the North.

It was my first essay at real travelling, and for a while I was possessed of the novelty and the interest of it.

For a few miles the trail was good and hard, for the Indians of the camp we had just left had trapped hereabouts and had built many rabbit-snares along the river. I remember, as the train passed by, I twice saw a pure white northern rabbit in these traps frozen to the hardness of stone. According to the courtesy of the wilderness, I took each from its trap, hung it upon the nearest spruce branch, re-shaped the wire noose, cleared the snow away from about the trap and went my way.

My men were walking briskly and paid no attention to my lagging steps; afterward I had to hurry to catch up with them. My broad snowshoes swung about very awkwardly; for though I had practised I was still unaccustomed to their use and I now found that I had gone upon the trail almost a stranger to the terrible fatigue of actual snowshoe travel. It was one thing to walk a mile or so at Quebec with a cup of tea at the end, and quite a different thing to keep up the paces of the trained *voyageur* of the wilderness. Nor did I ever attain anything like their perfect freedom in the use of the broad webs – the free rhythmic swing that seems to be an inheritance of birth and is not to be acquired by any amount of practice.

First published in *Scribner's Magazine*, May 1905.

Then the last of the rabbit-snares was passed, and with it the end of the beaten trail. It was as though the one little thread was snapped that had bound me to the life I had left behind. We left the creek bed and plunged directly into a thick bush of birch and spruce. Far up the steep ascent we followed the blaze of a winter trail marked on the trunks of the spruce and the birch. Some of the markings were old and almost covered with the spruce gum. Those on the birch were quite fresh and yellow, made by the Indians when they came on their last New Year's visit to the post.

Part way up the hill, I remember, we passed an Indian cache — four fifty-pound bags of flour covered with balsam boughs, and above this a pair of very broad snowshoes and some steel traps hung in a branch. An Indian from the camp had started on the long trail to Lake Mistassini, and had left these provisions for future use.

According to the laws of the wilderness, these caches are never touched by anyone else than their owners, for there is a code of honesty in these wilds that prevents any man from meddling with his neighbor's goods.

I struggled up the trail against the snow in company with the dogs, who were my special care. The poor animals pulled and tugged and strained and labored. They panted with red, hanging tongues. Their breath froze white on their heads in the gray cold, and from out of this frost looked their eyes, the one spark of black in their white faces. Frequently the sledge runner would catch on a projecting branch, the load would topple and roll over into the deep, unbroken snow, and it was then that one had to plunge into the drifted white and struggle waist-deep to right the sledge and push it back on the hard trail again.

I got one dog up to the top of the hill and saw a frozen lake spread out below me like the palm of a hand. The guides were far, far away — small spots of black against the yellow of the birch, breaking a trail in clouds of snow through the thick bush at the edge of the lake, and I had to go back for the other dog, that I could hear whining down the hill behind me.

This, as I said, was my first experience of heavy travelling — and it happened to be very heavy, indeed. Afterward I became more used to my snowshoes and was even able to take my turn in breaking trail.

To break trail is to pack with your snowshoes the soft and un-crusted snow into a more solid path, so that the dogs and the tobog-gans may be brought forward to where you make camp. Even the snowshoes, two feet in width, sink a foot or eighteen inches at every step. The snow crumbles and piles in on the top of the web, so that you have to tear each step with a wrench and a kick and a cloud of frozen white. You go forward, you rest, you go forward again, forcing your way laboriously through no one can say how many feet of snow. The weariness enters into the very marrow of your bones. The snowshoe strap moves back and forth just enough across the moose-hide moccasins to gall the foot to the flesh of the toes, the muscles across the in-step ache with knife-like cuts with every step as you lift the heavy weight of snow that covers the shoe.

I remember this first day out we stopped midway across the lake to rest. The guides dropped the tump-line from the forehead to their shoulders, cut some tobacco from a plug, rubbed it between their hands, and filled short black pipes. The dogs lay flat on the snow and bit and chewed at the solid lumps of ice that had gathered on the paws. With the handle of my axe I scraped from my snowshoes the frozen masses of ice that had gathered under my moccasins and were wearing blisters on my feet. We rested here only a few minutes, and then the bitter cold drove us on again, for no man dares to stop long in such a temperature.

This breaking trail is very picturesque to an outside observer. Oftentimes afterward, when, unencumbered, I had gone on ahead, I would stop and turn and watch the guides – black pygmies struggling through the boundless stretch of white, with their heavily loaded toboggans in great clouds of snow. With their shoulders thrust forward and their heads bent to the trail, they would swing along at an even stride across the level expanse of frozen snow, broken only by the thin line of trail stretching behind them off into the distance, and by the many still narrower tracks of the fox criss-crossing here and there on the smooth surface. Then as the men draw nearer, I hear the rasp and the clatter of the snowshoes sounding more and more distinct in the frigid silence as the broad webs scrape the one across the other; I hear the sharp click of the wooden tail as it strikes the rim of one shoe, slides off and sinks deep in the soft bed of white. The men come nearer in the great whirls of snow, ploughed up and thrown up by the broad snowshoes, in which they appear as black, unshapen masses. On them, on their backs, even on their fur caps, the snow hangs in little forms like mosaics. All about their faces, on the fur caps are halos of frozen breath.

One always stops for dinner at eleven o'clock, which is noon in the northland. The toboggans and sledges are drawn to the edge of the bordering spruce bush. Xavier clears the snow away from the lower branch of a small balsam and upon it hangs the tump-lines to prevent the snow from freezing on the moistened leather. The dogs are loosened; they shake themselves again and again in the very joy of their freedom; they walk around and around, making a little hard bed in the snow. They are very tired – they do not even notice the fresh tracks of a rabbit.

I unfasten my axe from the toboggan and fall to work with the guides. No one may stand idle. The clothing, damp from the terrible work of the morning, soon freezes on one's back in the biting air of thirty below. In the shelter of the bush a few yards from the edge of the lake, we tramp and pack the snow to a solid level. Many of the spruce-trees are cut and stripped of their branches. The green boughs are thrown in a semicircle on the packed surface and the small trunks are laid close together to prevent the fire melting its way into the snow. Xavier cuts a tall dead tamarack he had "marked" from the lake, and brings the tree down the hill on his shoulder. With one snowshoe resting on the log and the other sunk deep in the glistening white, he cuts and splits the dry wood into great lengths. Then from a small birch he strips some dry bark and starts a fire.

I bring the frying-pan and some provisions from the toboggans. It is bitter work in the biting cold of the open to unfasten the many strings that hold the loads, but no one thinks of complaining of cold in the wilderness or of listening to complaints. Skene goes well out on the lake and cuts a hole for water,* which he presently fetches, immediately freezing in a pail.

I slip my snowshoes, scrape the frozen bits of ice from the lacing, and thrust them tail down in the snow. With a little bundle of spruce boughs, I knock off the snow that has caked on the woollen tops of my moccasins and on the capote and sit down on the green boughs in the warmth of the fire and wait for the dinner.

I do not think I should like such food at home, but it is very appetizing there, after a hard morning of breaking trail: a pan of melted lard, a few pieces of fat pork cut from a frozen lump with an axe, a pail of boiled tea, thick and black. But we all gather close about the frying-pan very eagerly, and each of us dips his gillette** into the hot grease, which instantly hardens in the bitter cold. With

---

*It takes but a little while to do this, for the ice does not freeze in the farther North as it does with us. The weight of the snow upon the first fall freezing causes it to sink. The water oozes through the cracked ice and forms a layer of slush. Then comes another fall of snow and another layer of slush. This alternate formation of ice and slush continues throughout the winter and usually one has only to cut through a thick layer of ice to obtain a supply of half-frozen slushy snow. It answers very well for wilderness cooking.

**Some flour, water and baking soda are mixed together in the sack of flour. Then the lump is taken from the sack, put in the pan and fried. The surface is browned, very well indeed, but the inner portion is entirely uncooked, only becoming hard when it freezes while on the trail.

our knives we spread it and the cold lard thick upon the pieces of gillette and eat with a huge satisfaction, picking the pieces of fat pork out of the pan by way of tidbits. The tin-cups are filled many times with the black tea. It is bitter and scalding, but it acts like a tonic upon the tired body.

Such is a dinner cooked in the open of the northern wilderness, and we grew strong and rugged and lusty upon such faring. One day I remember we cooked such a dinner near an old Indian camp. Hanging on a post were nearly a dozen bear-skulls, silvery white against the green. Some tobacco still remained in the skulls, for the hunter as he hangs them up puts some in the nostril sockets. It is for luck and for the trapper who passes without a pipeful. Nearby were the smaller bones of the loon and the lynx. As you pass on the trail, you find many such piles of skulls and bones, swinging and rattling in the wind.

You stop walking a little before three o'clock and make camp for the night, which falls entirely dark by four. You make your camp in the shelter of some tall spruce-trees, whose tops lean always toward the south. You pack the snow and spread it deep with green boughs, and by the time you have put up the tent and have unloaded the provisions and belongings it is quite dark. A furious red fire is now blazing in the little sheet-iron stove, and then the terrible cold of the day is forgotten in its warmth and comfort. Your feet feel peculiarly light, and seated on a roll of blankets you light a pipe and watch the preparations for supper with a keen interest. The frying grease smells good and the pail of tea you think will hardly be sufficient for yourself alone. After the supper, Xavier, the cook, maybe sets to work making gillettes for future consumption, and after the gillettes are made and propped up in a row about the stove, the grease left from our own supper is mixed with some flour and fried like the gillettes, and so the dogs' meal is prepared. Indeed the only difference between the dogs' food and our own is that theirs is called pancakes and that ours is called gillettes.

En passant, the dogs are only fed once a day, and I do not think that they ever drink water – at least I never saw our dogs do so.

The northland night is very long and sometimes very lonely, but it is neither too long nor too lonely when the trail has been hard to break. For then the body is very weary and the simple preparations for the night soon follow the eating of supper. The moccasins are removed and the four or five pairs of thick "*habitant*" woollen socks are hung from the ridge pole of the tent to dry. The provisions and the sketching materials are piled about the walls of the tent to protect one's head from the bitter air. The Indian and the "breed" spread each a blanket on the bed of green and kneel a moment in prayer,

95

The Catch of a Fine
Marten; 1904.
Crayon and pastel; 9 x 17.

A Weasel Caught in a Mink Trap; 1904.
Mechanical reproduction of crayon drawing; 12 x 18.

A Dead-Fall for Mink and Marten; 1904.
Mechanical reproduction of crayon drawing; 18 x 12.

their bowed figures throwing great hunched shadows on the walls of the tent. Then they fold their coats for a pillow and roll up close together in a blanket.

Maybe you sit near the little stove for a while and smoke, but the fire gradually burns low and it grows cold in the tent. The night's allowance of half a candle burns out. A thin layer of ice forms over some tea left from supper. You wrap yourself, head and body, in three heavy blankets, pull a fur cap over your ears, move your swaddled feet to find the warmth of the dog's body. It is six o'clock and dark. Then you are asleep.

One day, an Indian family joined us and we travelled together. Tied on a toboggan almost under the high curved bow was a dark bronze baby, wrapped in a rabbit-skin coat. On its head was a cap made of the muskrat skin. In the same bundle with the baby was the family lard and a bag of flour. Besides these burdens, animate and otherwise, were two rabbits and a white ptarmigan, and the gun was securely fastened on the top of the load.

I became quite friendly with these Indians as we ploughed along together. The patriarch's name was Minn-e-goosh and it meant "Little Pine". He told me it had been a bad winter and the fall hunt had not brought him many skins.

His mother was of the party — an old Cree woman of some sixty years — and as we journeyed on we stopped many times upon the trail during the day and waited while she caught up with us.

"It's hard walking for her," I said to Minn-e-goosh.

"Yes," he said, "it's bad for some. The two boys there and the girl do well, but it's hard for an old woman to walk in snow like this."

"You are going far?" I asked.

"Yes; about two hundred miles — so — on the St. Maurice" — he pointed — "it's a good place for a hunt."

I can see the poor old squaw now, as she came swinging slowly along the trail to where we were and sat down to rest on one of the loads. In a pouch of red-cloth hanging across her back she carried a little black dog. She took from the same bag some tobacco and filled a pipe. Little white spots had begun to appear on her cheekbones where they were frozen, so she rubbed them with snow, while we waited and while the men scraped away the ice that had formed upon the iron runners of the sledges and upon the toboggans. Then we started on and she arose and followed us again.

We lived with this Indian family two days, and then our trails separated.

The Winter Harvesters

The object of my journey was to join company with the Indian trappers of the North; to become acquainted with them; to live their life and to learn their manners.

I have already told in another article how the Indians of a camp in which we lived had drawn for us a map of these uncharted and frozen regions upon a Hudson's Bay Company's brown paper bag. By means of this map we hoped to find the family camp of a certain trapper named Semo Mac-nee-call.

So we ploughed over the course thus mapped out for us through nine days of hard travel and seventy-five miles of unbroken snow. Then one morning we came upon several dead-falls along a portage – traps that had been set in times past for mink and marten. But they were abandoned and filled with snow and the bait had long since been eaten by the squirrels.

Xavier, who was breaking trail, pointed to them and remarked in a perfectly unconcerned manner, "Semo is not here."

A little beyond these traps and across the lake we came upon the abandoned camp – a few bare tent-poles, a broken iron pot hanging to the branch of a tree, and a pair of old worn-out snowshoes hanging beside the pot. This was all that was left of Semo Mac-nee-call's camp – all that we found of humanity after that long journey – a desolate empty camp in the midst of a frozen wilderness with night coming on.

The ridge-pole of the tent was inclined to a certain direction and there were some notches cut in the stick. This was full of meaning for Xavier, who read therefrom that Semo had gone to another trapping ground – a nine days' journey in the direction the stick pointed.

So the next morning we began again breaking trail in the direction pointed out by the tent pole.

During the latter part of this last voyage we found that our provisions were growing low, so we stopped several times, and while I sketched* the men set a score or so of rabbit-snares. By means of

---

*I had been told that it would be impossible to sketch out of doors in the midwinter Canadian woods, but before getting out from Quebec, I had made a small canvas tent with a glazed folding window. Whenever I found a picturesque subject I set up my tent, built a fire in a little stove that warmed it within, and sketched through the window, which I kept free of frost by covering it with a solution of glycerine and high-wine. It was quite comfortable sketching in this tent, if you kept the stove red hot. The Indians called it my "wabeno" because it looked like those huts in which the Indian conjurers perform their incantations.

Portrait of Semo-Mac-Nee-Call; 1904.
Crayon and pastel; 11 x 17.

these catches and the remainder of the provisions, we were just able to make the new camp of Semo in time to avoid the experiences of starvation.

One day about noon we turned a little promontory that thrust out upon the level, and suddenly there was Semo's camp across the smooth stretch, an eighth of a mile away. It stood upon a windswept bluff; three tents, standing clean cut against the white hill behind. The smoke arose straight and thin from the stove-pipes and my heart warmed more than I can say toward this one little cluster of human life found after all these two hundred weary miles of snow. There was not a sign of life to be seen, but as we started across the lake the dogs commenced barking, and in a moment the Indians came pouring out of the tents, and stood upon the bluff and watched our approach.

The three tents belonged to Semo, Semo's brother, and a half-breed named Jerome la Croche. In a little we reached the encampment and Semo and Xavier, who were old friends, welcomed one another.

We stayed in this camp four or five days and I made several sketches. I set up my *wabeno* and the Indians came and watched me as I worked. One day whilst I was busy sketching some skins and trapping paraphernalia hanging from a rack, a boy managed to squeeze inside. He watched me intently, standing so close to the red-hot stove that he singed the cloth tops of his moccasins. He made no comment of any sort and, after a while, he suddenly left and went into one of the tents. Presently he came out and hung very carefully upon the rack another mink-skin and a big trap. Then he came in and watched me again.

One afternoon I paid a visit to Semo's tent. They prepared a place for me and I sat down. Across from where I sat, Semo's old mother, a Cree Indian, was seated on a caribou-skin, making a gill-net for winter fishing in the lakes. As the net grew she wound it about a stake that was driven through the floor of green boughs into the snow beneath. She stopped when I offered her some tobacco and filled a pipe. Then, being of a thrifty disposition, she brought out another blackened bowl from a little bag, filled it also, and put it in the pocket of her blue woollen skirt for future use.

Semo's wife was skinning a mink and Semo sat and smoked and watched her from the independent height of his superiority. She had fastened the head of the mink to her moccasin with a piece of old ribbon and was stripping off the furry skin. When she had finished her work, she handed the skin to Semo; he inserted two flat sticks and then a third, which, acting as a wedge, stretched the pelt taut and flat. He cut some notches in the sides of the wooden form, pulled down the long furry strips, and fastened the sharp toes in the little cuts. I sat and watched, smoking the while.

It was very pleasant to rest thus in this one little oasis of humanity in all that great white desert, but the weather was cold, and only a little trapping was being done. So we remained only for four or five days before going upon our way.

The next camp we visited was presided over by an ex-chief of the Montagnais Indians, who rejoiced in the Hibernian patronymic of Patrick Cleary. Because of his former greatness among them, the Indians and half-breed trappers looked up to him with immense respect and even veneration. They always addressed him or referred to him as M'sieur or M'sieur Cleary. There were two families in this camp — six people in all. Patrick Cleary told me that I was the first white man who had ever visited his camp in winter. And during the week or two that I was there we became really intimate.

He was a tall, thin man with big bones, and he was very dark even for a half-breed. He was unusually intelligent, and better educated than any man I had seen since I had left the post.

Day after day I went with him over the trail examining the traps; I watched him build dead-falls on the snow, and set steel traps in the water. He told me many things of the lore of the wilderness, and even opened his heart concerning his childish superstitions and beliefs. He would stop at my tent in the morning and ask if I would like to go with him over his traps — a journey sometimes of two or three days. Upon these occasions — companions in the silent wilderness — we would talk intimately and he would tell me tales of magic and of conjuring mysteries, sometimes by camp-fire, sometimes in the still whiteness of the daytime as we sat smoking together. I half believe he himself was a conjurer, but I did not like to ask him if he were, and he did not volunteer to tell me.

Going the rounds of the traps is a routine that never varies, and yet it possesses an ever-changing interest — the chance of a catch, the hazards of the wilderness, the constant variations of snow and cold, the wilderness of the solitude perfumed with the ever-pervading odor of spruce and balsam.

How vivid are the impressions of such a day. You are awakened in the bitter darkness of the early morning by the sound of the camp dogs moving among the frozen pails of refuse. You hear their padding footsteps passing this way and that outside of the tents and the brushing of their bodies against the canvas walls. Then you hear the sound of chopping wood where someone is at work in the starlight. One of the men stirs and rises in the darkness. The tent is bitter cold with everything frozen as hard as iron. You hear the man

A Day's Catch of Fine Fur; 1904.
Crayon and pastel; 10½ x 17.

fumbling around in the darkness for the matches, and presently he strikes one and lights a candle, and in the sudden light I see it is Xavier Gill. Presently he begins chopping the wood for the stove and his big round shadow moves uncouthly and grotesquely about the walls as the flame of the candle wavers in the draught of the cold air. He makes a fire, and in a moment the flame is roaring up the stove-pipe, which gradually becomes a dull red with the gushing heat.

Gill stands with his back to the stove and presently the other man rises and joins him. Then you yourself move reluctantly in your warm swaddling of furs and with some effort crawl out into the bitter cold and join the others around the stove. None of you speaks, but each absorbs the scanty heat in silence. But by and by, warmed to some return of life, you peep out of the tent; the sky is like black crystal, the stars shining with an incredible effulgence. From the stove-pipes of the other tents rockets of flame are gushing up into the air; showers of sparks rise up into the night high overhead — hover, waver, and then sink dwindling upon the tent and the surrounding snow. You look at the thermometer hanging against a tree and see by the light of a match that it is forty degrees below zero. By this time the smell of cooking is filling the silent frozen spaces of the darkness and you re-enter the tent to hug again the warmth of the stove with a huge appetite for the rude breakfast of melted grease and gillettes.

The day is just dawning when the tent flap is raised and Patrick Cleary's face looks in. He asks if you have had your breakfast and if you are ready to go with him. You join him outside, twist your feet into your snowshoes, and are off into the early gray of the day with dog and toboggan loaded with the provisions for the voyage.

Presently the strong March sun rises and shines on the blinding snow; the dazzling light pierces the eyes like needles and you feel the glow of the sun warm upon your back. By and by you pass from the glittering radiance of the lake into the cold vivid purple shadows of the bush. All about on the frozen white are thousands of little tracks like the veins of a leaf, and the snow is packed hard beneath the lower branches of the spruce, where the rabbits have been feeding.

Just within the bush you come upon the tracks of two otters, ploughed deep across the trail. You follow these tracks; they lead over the crest of a hill, down the other side, and finally disappear in the open water of a very narrow stream. Patrick cuts some stakes and drives them into the creek bottom, leaving an opening in the

The Edge of the Wilderness; 1904.
Crayon; 11 x 17.

The Trapper; 1927.
Oil; 24 x 30.

Indian Family at Tent Entrance; 1911.
Lantern slide and hand tinting by F. E. Schoonover.

The Trading Post at Long Lake; 1925.
Oil; 28 x 36.

The Bronze Face of the Chief is Lifted; 1912.
Oil; 30 x 42.

A Friendly Game; 1904.
Oil; 20 x 30.

Dickering with the Factor; 1912.
Oil; 30 x 21.

centre in which he set a trap, fastening the end of the chain to a pole. Always he handles the trap with a little forked stick, never touching his hand to the steel. This trap set, you return to your trail and Patrick blazes a tree, marking the location of the snare.

By and by you find two martens, each frozen as hard as stone in its dead-fall. Each of them is put into a canvas bag which the hunter carries over his shoulder. The traps are set with baits, and you resume your journey.

You go five miles without finding any more catch, and then you stop to rest and to light a pipe.

After a while you find the big clumsy tracks of a lynx; you follow them for a great distance along the bed of a stream, sometimes losing them in the bush, sometimes finding them again. By and by you come to a tree, scarred and scratched from the catch of many foregone years. Here Patrick lays aside his bag and unslings his axe; the dog lies down on the snow, panting with lolling tongue, and you take out your pipe, fill it, and get it going.

He builds a trap called a *cabane*. It is like a little house, open in front; the back wall is the tree, the side walls are built of stakes driven into the snow, and the top is roofed over with green balsam boughs. He makes it of both old and green wood and the roof he fashions like the drooping branch of a balsam.

Cleary takes an indescribable something from a wooden bottle – a vile smelling object made from certain parts of the beaver and musk-rat; he rubs it on a piece of birch bark. This he fastens in a splinter of wood and sticks it up in the snow inside the *cabane*. Behind the stick he props up a dead rabbit. He covers the steel trap with the tender ends of the spruce and fastens the chain to a heavy pole. He builds eight of these traps along the river and you watch him and smoke.

It is noon by now. Cleary makes a fire and boils some tea and you eat a dinner of cold lard and gillettes. Then you smoke and talk and smoke again.

Such is the way these folk of the North gather their winter harvest. All about them is the frozen solitude, and the breath of the wilderness enters so into their every fibre that I believe they would pine and die like the wild creatures of the woods and streams if they were transplanted from their native desolation to another life. I lived the life for only about two weeks, but I think of it now over and over again when I am by myself, and it will never cease to be a vital part of my memory.

When I quit the camp of Cleary I turned my face once again

toward the civilization from which I had emerged, to leave behind me all that rude, free, untrammelled existence.

The last person I saw was Patrick Cleary. We were well out on the lake where the trail turned sharply, and I stopped for a last look at the camp I was leaving. On the bank, quite above the lake, was an Indian, a black silhouette against the white hill. I waved him a good-by. He raised his hand, held it so a moment, then turned toward his tent. Then the bend of the trail hid the camp and the thread that had bound me to a different life and a different people was cut in twain.

The Fur Harvesters

Silently from out of the big, mysterious shadows they came to stare at the *Shaganoosh* – white men from the rails that ran, far to the south, a steel band from ocean to ocean. Indians – *Nitchies* of the North – had appeared on the edge of the trail.

"*Bo' jou, bo' jou, Nitchie!*"

"*Bo' jou, Shaganoosh!*"

We did not stop to look at them; we did not dare. The mosquitoes were about us in clouds, and, moreover, the uncertain light that precedes the rising of the moon made it necessary to fight our way through the three miles of swamp portage. They stepped back as we passed along, watched us for a moment, and then disappeared in the shadows, going along a moose runway to their camp somewhere in the woods.

We struggled along for a while, and then rested the canoe and packs on windfalls that were across the trail. We were too weary to talk. Pipes were filled and started, to keep away the bugs. These were terrible, for it was fly-time – June, and early in the month.

Part way across this three-mile trail there rested a little company of three adventurers – a Canadian, an Irishman, and an American – who were pushing northward into the Hudson Bay country. This carry was known as the "Height of Land" portage. It was the thread-like highway that carried the *voyageur* across the water divide of Canada. But the name was a misnomer hereabout, for the watershed was a great swamp, with an elevation of only a few feet. To the south of the Height of Land the waters found their way slowly to the great Lake Superior. These were the rivers and lakes of the sportsman. To the north lay a vast and intricate water route to James Bay, that had as yet no certain topographical birth save that made by the hand of the Indian map-maker on a piece of birch-bark.

It was still one of the great, wild trapping-grounds of Canada, and it was our purpose to venture north into the very heart of the Cree and Ojibway country, to watch the coming of the fur-brigades to the posts and see the trading of the winter's catch at the factors' stores. The fur-hunters come to the posts early in June, so our journey northward had become a race toward a picturesque gathering-place of the fur-harvesters. Thus, with the rest of a pipe, we made ready to labor again along the wretched swamp portage.

First published in *Harper's Magazine*, October 1912.

The north end of the Height of Land portage leads into the head of Gaining Ground River – and a cloud of mosquitoes. It was good to see the river, a sluggish stream that flowed north to a great inland lake and a Hudson Bay post, but the countless thousands of flies were discouraging. Our faces, necks, and hands were already in a pitiable condition.

Packs were placed in the canoe, and the entire load roped in so that nothing would be lost in a rapid in case of accident. John, the cook, crawled in over the dunnage, leaving a trail of mud over everything; I took my place in the middle; and Fred, the Canadian – a prince among canoe-men – gently shoved off and took his place in the stern. We pushed hard at the paddles, and the flies were soon left astern. At the end of the eighteen miles of slow-flowing river was a Hudson Bay post and some civilization. The canoe passed from the great patches of moonlight into the dense shadows of the tall jack-pines. Within these, two rapids were run, with nothing more than the sound of the rushing waters for a guide. The element of chance was not in the waters alone. Twice we passed long poles covered with the bleached skulls of the bear and bones of the moose. Bits of ribbon and rags hung from the very top; tall and ghostly they stood, mute offerings to the Wendigo for a good hunt.

Mile after mile, along this wilderness highway, we passed. The great shadows of the night and the vast silence of the North country seemed to brood upon us. There was no sound save the steady dip of three paddles, and the curl of the water as it followed the blades. Presently, however, from out the shadows of the distance emerged a little meadow-like spot, a clearing of but a few feet square. As we drew near, the moonlit patch separated into detail. Two birch-bark canoes were drawn up on the bank; just back of them was a bark-built wigwam with a smudge fire smoldering at the entrance. We stopped paddling and let the canoe drift toward the bank. This was a touch of wild life that had existed hereabout for two hundred years. We looked a long time at the Indian home and at the details about it – the rabbit-blanket, the old winter toboggan, and snow-shoes. Indeed, the whole history of the struggle between nature and the fur-harvesters might be written around those few necessities of travel in the Northland, that have not been changed one whit since the Hudson's Bay Company was incorporated in 1670. Presently Fred called aloud:

"Bo' jou! Bo' jou! Bo' jou!" And then again, as if no one had heard, "Bo' jou! Nitchie!"

Presently a blanket that covered the wigwam entrance was pulled back, and a tangled mass of black hair and a face appeared.

Then, after a long look and much rubbing of the eyes, a dark form pulled itself from out of the folds of the blanket, and a shirt-clad Indian stood before us. He was very careful to get into the smoke of the smudge fire, as he was possessed of but scanty protection from the mosquitoes. Fred asked him in Ojibway how far it was to the Long Lake post.

"Oh, 'bout one mile," he replied.

We thanked him in a light-hearted way, for what was one mile to the many we had paddled and portaged for that day and half of the night? So we dipped our blades and left. But the joy of one mile to the Hudson Bay post was short-lived. One mile became two, then three. After an hour's paddling we decided that the Indian had a very poor idea of distance. We found out afterward that whenever the portage, a lake, or some known place is not over a half-day's journey distant the Indian calls it about a mile.

So we were looking about for some place to rest for the few remaining hours of the night, when the canoe passed over some floats that marked the fish-nets of the Indians. Several of these nets were crossed. Then we came to a great stretch of water. It was Long Lake. On a rocky point, near an old wharf and storehouse, we made a landing. Across the lake a single light shone out from the Long Lake post. It was but a mile away and suggested many comforts, but we were worn out and unable to go farther. The canoe had been placed in the water at dawn, and it was now past midnight – a quarter after one. A fire was made on a flat rock, an old Peterborough boat with "H.B.C." painted on its bow was pulled up as a wind-break, and we rolled ourselves in the blankets; then we were asleep.

"White man, no tent, sleep late."

As we crawled from under the damp blankets there passed by the rocky point an old Indian and his wife in their birch-bark canoe. It was not so very late. The sun was scarce a paddle-blade's width above the line of purple that marked the distant shore of the lake, and against this narrow ribbon of distance a string of small white dots marked the buildings of the Hudson's Bay Company. Quite close, and on the same rocky shore where we had camped for the night, were some log buildings. From the chimney of one of these a thin line of smoke rose against the sky. With that evidence of life near at hand, we loaded the canoe and proceeded along the shore in search of a ready-made breakfast.

We were not long in finding it. The buildings we had seen were those of a great French company, the competitor of the Hudson's Bay Company. We found the factor in the store. He told us that breakfast was over. But that did not matter, for such is the great hospitality of the traders of the North that nothing seems too great a trouble. The factor took us to his log-house close by the store, and told his Indian wife that three white men had arrived from the south, and that they were to have some breakfast. So the woman moved about stealthily in her moccasined feet, preparing a breakfast and watching us the while. Presently food was placed before us – food, not of the trout of the lake and streams, but of canned meat, stove-made bread, and, best of all, a can of peaches that made their way north over the same two hundred miles of trail that we had traveled.

While we were eating breakfast the factor told us that he had not been across the lake for several days, and did not know if the chief had arrived. Some of his own Indians were in, but not all.

So, with the quest of the trip still in doubt, we set forth, and the four or five white spots that we had seen from across the lake gradually grew and outlined themselves into the buildings of the Hudson's Bay Company's post and the church. Strung along on the point and upon a bare, rock-crested hill were many teepees and tents.

We brought our canoe to this wharf. Several Indian boys who had been playing with bows and arrows stopped and watched us unload the canoe, lift it from the water, carry it up the bank, and put it within the company's fence. Blankets were spread to dry, for we were to remain a day or two. This was a post of the greatest fur-trading company in the world, and it was here that all trails led, even our own, to meet that of the fur brigade. Had these forest people arrived? It was to be a simple "Yes" or "No" that was to be told us in a short while by the factor himself.

He appeared in the doorway of the store just as we were returning to the wharf to bring up our dunnage, and invited us within. Later, we went out from the store, along the narrow plank walk to the house close by. There was a long bench on the porch, and we sat down. Beyond the porch was the fenced inclosure of the company, with its flag-pole and fur-press. A narrow footpath for the Indians followed the fence, and beyond it the ground sloped abruptly to the lake and the small wharf. In the distance was the lake, the great waterway of the fur-harvesters. By way of answer to the question that had been uppermost in our minds for many days, the factor turned and pointed with the stem of his pipe.

"Do you see that bit of an open spot at the far end of the lake? That's where a river, the Kenogami, puts out to the north. And that's the way a good many of the trappers come to the post. Up that river, into the lake, and straight across to the point there where you see those half-dozen wigwams."

The Factor's Wife and Child; 1912.
Ink and Watercolor; 14½ x 18.

We asked him if he happened to be looking for any such trappers that day.

"Oh yes," he said, "'most any time today or tomorrow. I'm looking for the chief of the tribe here and his party. He's a few days late this spring."

It was on the day following that the chief came. The factor had been watching the north end of the lake with his glass. About an hour before sunset he turned to us and said, "The chief and the canoes are coming."

Presently we saw them – bits of yellow and brown, a tiny flash of light from the paddle-blade, a mass of rich golden color in the light of the setting sun. The news of the chief's coming had permeated every nook and cranny of the post. From the teepees on the bare, rocky hill, from the low land back of the company's buildings, from the bush and the water's edge, came the Indians to greet their chief and those that followed. It was a procession such as you might see nowhere in the whole world but in the Hudson Bay country – Cree and Ojibway, trappers and women, children and papooses, half-tamed husky dogs. Every year as far back as any trail led to the post the Indians have gathered in just such manner to greet the chief and the trappers as they come sweeping up the river and across the lake to their summer camping-ground.

Now the canoes have crossed part of the lake. You make a count and discover there are nine – all birch-bark. They seem to be low in the water, and as they draw nearer, with the perfect sweep of their paddles that is a matter of inheritance and not to be acquired, you see that these frail boats of bark carry the trapper, his family, his hunt, all his worldly possessions, and his husky dogs. Presently you witness a gradual change in the scattered formation of the nine canoes. They had been approaching pretty much as their fancy chose, but now they slowly form into single file, a long line of golden bark, and at its head, in the bow of the canoe, rides the chief. His paddle rests across the canoe, and he searches out each member of the company with his bead-like eyes. He has all the dignity and the silent poise of an Indian, for his wife does the paddling.

Now they stop their water-craft; only that of the chief drifts slowly toward the shore. There is a little movement of the heads of those on the bank as they look long and intently at each of their kind floating there on the water. But there is no greeting, no sound, not a single movement of the hand. The canoes and their human loads might be those of a strange tribe. There is no longer even a subdued murmuring.

You can hear the scraping of the chief's birch-bark against the long water-grass as it floats over the shallows. When the chief is within a canoe's length of the shore, he rises, puts the paddle-blade in the shallow water, and rests on the end of it. The bronze face, golden in the fading light, is lifted in proud scrutiny of his friends on the bank, but still there is no sign of recognition or of a bond of friendship. Presently he removes his paddle, and the woman pushes the canoe slowly to the shore. The chief steps out.

Then follows as strange a greeting as one may wish to see. The chief goes to each member of the tribe on the bank, grasps his right hand, and, looking straight into his eyes, holds the hand for what seems to be fully a minute. No word is spoken. The mask-like face does not change one whit. The chief goes to each member of the tribe and greets him with this solemn hand-shake. Then he steps back, leans on his paddle, and watches the other canoes come to the shore and empty themselves of their human freight and the precious loot of the forests. Such is the manner in which a chief of the fur-hunters lands in far-north Canada.

Upon occasion there is a priest to invoke a blessing upon the canoe flotilla before they land. For two hundred years these comings to the post have been as regular as the coming of spring itself. For that time and more the Indian has given his life to add his little pile of furs to the forty or fifty million dollars' worth that yearly go to the big world and the fair lady. The winter's catch is his very life; it keeps him facing death in the vast white silence of the frozen months, and calls him to the post with the soft winds of the South.

Now that the chief has landed, there is no longer the impressive stillness. The wild, husky dogs jump from the canoes and come splashing to the shore. Some are tied about the muzzle with a thong, and a bit of rag holds one foreleg in a kind of sling, to prevent them running wild. The men gather in groups while the women unload the canoes and pile on the bank a collection of clothing, cooking utensils, and brand-new papooses. There are muzzle-loading guns, beaded powder and cap bags, and yellow powder-horns. A pile of rabbit-blankets is topped by a something covered with birch-bark and wrapped about and about by caribou thongs. You notice a number of little bundles, and are told that these carefully wrapped affairs contain the forest loot of the fur-hunters. Within the strips of bark are hundreds of dollars' worth of raw pelts, from muskrat to the silver fox. Yet they are thrown about with no more care than if they contained nothing at all.

Like some magic city, now rise about you the pyramids of poles and sections of birch-bark that go to make the Indian's home. The loot and litter on the bank is claimed and thrown within its shelter.

No Word is Spoken; 1912.
Ink and watercolor; 15½ x 20.

The Chief Grasps the Hand of Each in Turn; 1912.
Ink and watercolor; 15½ x 20.

Then the fires are started. They burn, a row of bright spots along the newly settled point of land. You look into the west; the sun has long since dipped beneath the lake.

On the morrow the hunter sits about his bark home and at his own convenience takes his bales of fur to the company store. The morning passes, and then noon. A meal is prepared and eaten. Then presently the hunters begin to stir about and gather their packs and take them to the store.

You follow, and watch the trading of the fur from the vantage-point of the counter. The Indians come into the big, square room of the company, seat themselves on the counters, on the benches, and on the floor. A few of the women with papooses, and a boy or two, help overcrowd the desirable places. When all have got into the store, the chief goes to the counter and shakes hands with the factor, the bookkeeper, and the outpost factor, in the same solemn manner that he greeted the members of the tribe the previous day. Then he has a long and seemingly important conversation with the *Ogima* (factor). The great *Ogima* is moved by the chief's earnest appeal, and he produces from somewhere beneath the counter a cap with a patent-leather visor. He hands it to the Indian, who removes his own tattered headgear and proudly places the cap in its place. Across the front of the cap, in tinseled finery, is woven the name "CHIEF." The brave hunter now has his badge of authority. Throughout the summer he will wear the cap, and his people will call him *Newatchegejick-wabe* (the Great Chief).

The factor now enacts the prelude to a dramatic play that proceeds almost without words. To each of the hunters he hands a plug of cheap, black tobacco and a package of sulphur matches – all a gift from the great trading company. Immediately pipes are filled with the sticky tobacco cut from the plug. Nothing is said while the pipe of welcome is smoked. It is a very serious matter, the smoking of a pipeful of that tobacco. It requires constant attention and the entire bundle of matches. Finally the chief knocks his pipe free from ashes and puts it carefully away. Then he cuts the caribou thongs from one of the bark-covered bales, and spreads upon the counter a pile of raw furs – his own personal hunt, made since New Year's Day. The factor begins at the top of the chief's pile and first counts two hundred and fifty muskrats. He thrusts his hand in each pelt, judges of the value, and gives the amount to the bookkeeper, who sits close by. Each pelt in the catch is examined carefully and passed to the outpost factor, who piles them on the counter.

You watch the hunter and the company's agent. No word passes between them. The cunning chief watches the factor as a lynx would a rabbit. His sharp, bead-like eyes do not miss a movement. He follows every motion of the sensitive fingers, trained after many years' practice to perfect and fair judgment of a pelt. The hunter hears him say, although he does not understand a word, as he moves his hand over a glossy pelt,

"One fine otter, usual high price, twenty-five.

"One mink, three; one mink, five; another fine otter, same high price."

And so he continues, until finally you hear the chief's spring catch amounts to two hundred and fifty dollars. The factor touches the Indian on the shoulder and tells him it is a fine hunt.

The chief then, as is befitting his station, trades in the pelts of all who made the hunt with him. He places on the counter a small pile of skins, his daughter's hunt — thirty muskrats — for which she receives a credit of about seven dollars. Then there follows an exceptionally good hunt of an Indian who has been blacklisted because, as the bookkeeper says, his debt is of three years' standing and amounts to six hundred dollars. But the magnificent lot of fur that is topped by a fine silver fox, the prize catch of all hunters, has brought his indebtedness to only twelve dollars. And in such a manner the hunt of the tribe is traded to the great company.

On the counter are thousands of dollars' worth of furs, mink and marten, muskrat and sable; the dark fur of the otter melts into that of the black bear. The whole dark, soft, furry mass is dotted here and there by the white of the ermine. Back of this pile of skins, hanging from nails and carrying the mass of furs to the very beams of the room, are the lynx and the foxes — the red, the "cross," and the silver gray, the latter each a small fortune in itself, and worth much over a thousand dollars apiece in the big market.

At one time, however, a single skin had no such value. A flintlock gun was worth fifteen to twenty beaver-skins; a white blanket, eight; an ax, one pound in weight, three beaver-skins; a half-pint of gunpowder, one; ten balls, one; tobacco fetched one beaver-skin per foot of "Spencer's Twist"; and rum marked "not very strong", two beaver-skins per bottle. Such were the prices demanded by the great company about the year 1775.

But your trapper, who sits close by, knows very little of the history of traders, and less of the outside world. The post is his great metropolis. He flocks to it in the spring to spend his all in riotous living. He is impatient, as are all the others, for the trading to be finished and his credits established, for then it is that you see the wiry bronze man, who has successfully fought the frozen wilderness at fifty below, become as a little child before a piece of cloth that boasts of a crude green, a yellow, or a red. He boasts of taking a bear single-handed and without the use of a gun, yet he gives that same pelt for gaudy ribbons, a box of colored thread, and some patent medicines. The motto of the company, *"Pro pelle cutum"* (a skin for a skin), is a true one.

The trading is done. The lighthearted trappers depart with their cheap finery. With the passing of the last, the factor closes the door and turns the key. In the quiet of the late afternoon the pelts of fur — some of them worth more than their weight in gold — are carried to the store-room above. There, under the shingled roof and the adz-marked rafters, are skins upon skins, great piles of them that mount shoulder-high into the dimly-lighted attic. Upon these the factor and his two assistants toss armful upon armful; and when all of the pelts brought in that day have been added to those traded in the New Year season, it is a sight to turn the mind of the fair lady.

We marveled at the wealth of the business that had never been cornered nor formed into a trust.

"This post," remarked the factor, in a laconic manner, "is noted for its rich shipment of furs; this is nothing unusual."

He closed and carefully locked the door that had opened to our vision only a glimpse of the vast riches of the northern wilderness. We descended the steep stairway, the great door of the company's store was opened, and we passed out into the twilight. The day of trading was ended. The post will not see its like again for another year.

The glow of twilight slowly merges into deep shadows and silvery lights. A full moon rises. It bathes with a soft green light the buildings of the Hudson's Bay Company and the teepees of the Indians. Perhaps you leave the factor's house, cross the small fenced inclosure, and find your way up the rocky hillside, dotted with the many wigwams of the Ojibways. The Indians step outside their homes to gaze after you. At the top of the hill, where a cross silhouettes against the sky, you sit down and look about. The surface of Long Lake is calm and placid. Not a breath of air mars the reflections of the stars and the thin line of the distant shore. Columns of smoke from the smudge fires rise straight and thin. The women move about making the crude shelters as tight as possible. Presently, when the teepee is quite full of smoke, the blanket will be drawn across the one opening, and the strange, silent folk will be sheltered for the night.

Almost at your very feet there lies brooding a nomadic race whose life is a great tragedy. There is nothing to show for the trails that run from the post like silver threads into the unbroken wilderness of the

North. They live and die. A little weather-bleached cross of wood marks their grave, and a friendly Indian hangs upon it a rosary and a few leaves from the Balm of Gilead. But in the big city of a winter's evening you may see his hunt, all plucked and groomed and fashioned into shape for the season of social struggle.

A black shadow that comes along the rocky path draws nearer and takes a place by you on the big rock. It is the chief. He knows no English, so by way of establishing a common bond of friendship you pass him your tobacco that is all ready for smoking and does not require cutting from the plug. The chief seems very much pleased at being honored with so remarkable a smoking mixture, and the head of five hundred Indians sits content with his pipe and the stranger.

You look hard at this chief of the trappers. Far out across the deep waters of Long Lake he gazes. His head sinks a little between the broad shoulders. A long, wiry strand of black hair falls over the high cheek-bone and is lost in the black of the handkerchief about his neck. His big, sinewed hand grasps the pipe as it would an ax-handle. Across the back of his hand are three long parallel scars. Perhaps within that breast there stirs the mystery of the unknown, of the legends and myths of the Northland, things hidden from one who only brushes against the fabric of their unfathomable life, but the chief brings himself to the commonplace things of every-day life. He unfastens the strings of his newly acquired factory-made shoes and removes them.

A sigh of relief escapes him. No doubt he longs for the soft caribou moccasins that have been part and parcel of his make-up for the last half-year. He examines the hard leather foot-gear as best he can in the moonlight, and glances at the heavy shoes of the stranger. Verily the ways and customs of the white man are a mystery to him! He drops the shoes and then turns wistfully toward the village of bark. From somewhere in the distance comes the sound of a harmonica. The chief gathers up his shoes and patters down the hillside to find the teepee and its musician.

Bringing the Outdoors In

I really don't know why I started to number my pictures. It is so unusual for an artist to have a system of any sort, that it seems strange indeed to realize, not that at Chadds Ford, Pa., on August 7, 1899, I started a sort of a daybook, but that each illustration of any importance painted since that time has had its number and its entry. The time put upon each picture has also been faithfully kept, and the size and kind of canvas or material used. There are many little charcoal, pen and pencil drawings that have not been included in this numbering process.

This little daybook is before me now. Turning back I find it says that drawing number one was made for a book by Everett T. Tomlinson. About a year ago when the number reached 940, I began to wonder what sort of a picture I would be painting for 1,000. Now there isn't anything magic about that number 1,000, but it sort of marks a long period of work – a kind of monument that one erects for himself.

The more I thought about it, the more I wanted that thousandth picture to be one of the open, an out-of-doors illustration – perhaps something of Canada. I even planned this number 1,000 fellow to be a subject all of my own – not connected with a story – but when number 995 came, and then number 999, I realized that I was so busy there just wasn't time to stop and make a special 1,000, so I let the picture come as it happened to in natural progression.

Connie Morgan's Luck

So it was that "Connie and 'Merican Joe" drew the big round number. And it really was very fortunate that Connie came along just then for I painted my own Canadian woods life into the illustration that goes with James B. Hendryx's story, "The Trail in the Snow".

I had real fun painting this picture. It was not so hard to imagine myself Connie, and for my Indian guide, Xavier Gill, to be 'Merican Joe. And the camp that you see in the illustration was just the same sort of a "one-night home" I have made many times in the far northland. And the title of the story, "The Trail in the Snow", is a very

---

First published in *The American Boy*, May 1921.

View of the Wabeno; 1903.
*Photograph by
F. E.Schoonover.*

Schoonover raising
"Howard Pyle School of
Art" banner at campside;
1904.

Left:
Schoonover fishing
through ice; 1904.

Top right:
Xavier Gill on snow-
shoes; 1904.
*Photograph by
F. E. Schoonover.*

Bottom right:
Schoonover and
Ojibway Chief at
Hudson's Bay Post,
Long Lake; 1911.

suggestive one. For the artist has made many many hundreds of miles of trail-tracks in the snows of Canada to gather material not only for the Connie stories, for Laurie York Erskine's Northwest Mounted Police stories, and James Willard Schultz's stories of Indians and trappers and traders, but for many others that he hopes to paint.

Four Winter Months in the Wild

But I did not always have this true and first hand working knowledge of the woods life. Years ago, I had been painting a great many pictures of Indians, Canadians, trappers, half-breeds and voyagers of the North. I really knew nothing about them. All the pictorial knowledge that I had was gathered from illustrations other men had made of outdoor subjects and from photographs and worded descriptions of the woods people.

The more I worked on the out-of-doors pictures the more I came to realize that an artist couldn't make true illustrations of trappers and Indians without knowing something about them. So I made up my mind to finish the work I had on hand and then go to Canada.

I remember very well the day that I rushed into Howard Pyle's studio and told him what I was going to do. He was very enthusiastic about it all and gave me every assistance to prepare for the trip.

In November of 1903 I arrived in Quebec. I established myself in a little town of Cap Rouge, some ten or twelve miles from the capital of the province. As the trip that I had in mind was going to be a winter one, I had first to acquire the knack of using snowshoes. This was accomplished by walking the ten miles or more into the city and back to Cap Rouge. After two or three weeks of this practice, I made ready in earnest and started, with a full-blooded Montagnais Indian, a half-breed and a dog team, for the Hudson's Bay Post at Pointe Bleue, Canada.

I broke trail early in December and came out to civilization the latter part of March. In the course of that four months' trip of over a thousand miles of snowshoe travel, I stopped with many Indian families, living with some for a week or more. I went over the trap line with skilled hunters, until I found out something of the ways of the trappers. Later I built my own traps and caught the fur-bearing animals of the North.

I was especially interested a few months ago when I read, in the manuscript of Mr. Hendryx's story entitled "Bait – and a Bear", a detailed description of a trap which the Indian, 'Merican Joe, made to catch the *loup cervier* or lynx.

It was the first time I had ever read a written or printed description of that particular kind of a trap, but, having "been there" I recognized at once that Mr. Hendryx had also "been there" and knew what he was talking about. To verify my recollection I got out the diary I kept on that winter trip in Canada and found not only a description similar to Mr. Hendryx's but a sketch of such a trap which I had made out there in the open when (as a notation at the top of the diary page shows) the temperature was 42 degrees below zero. So I had no difficulty in drawing this little known trap, with its bait and snare, all set for the lynx.

Sketching in 50 Below Weather

Such sketches, made in the open, have been of very great value to me in all my painting. I was busy making sketches all the time. Before going into this sub-arctic country, I had been told that it would be impossible to sketch in the mid-winter woods. But I overcame that difficulty by inventing a small sketching tent.

This small canvas affair was three feet by four and about seven or eight feet high. It was held erect by the use of four poles. The little tent had a folding window with four panes of glass in it. When I wanted to make a sketch of an animal caught in a trap or some Indian teepee or a fine bit of the trail, I set up the tent, put the little window in its place and covered the glass with a solution of glycerine and alcohol. This prevented the frost from collecting on the glass and made it possible for me to see the thing I wanted to draw.

There was a small sheet-iron stove, put on four green posts, set right in the doorway of the sketching house. I straddled this, after wrapping my legs with old flour bags and pieces of an old blanket. The tent was so small that there was no room for the back leg of the easel, so a small hole was cut in the rear wall of the canvas and the leg thrust through out into the snow.

All the pictures were made with colored crayons. It was too cold to use oil colors. I tried it once but the paint froze on the pallette.

Whenever an unusually fine animal was caught in a deadfall, I asked the Indian to leave for a few hours. I would hurry back to the camp, load the sketching house and stove on a toboggan, harness up a dog, and snowshoe along the trail to the trap. There the house would be set up and I would go to work. Many days it was fifty below zero when I was working, but there was lots of birch and tamarack for fuel and I was quite comfortable.

The Indians called this sketching tent the "Wabeno" because it looked like the little devil house in which their medicine men perform their incantations.

Building the Lynx Cabane; 1904.
Crayon and pastel; 17½ x 11½.

Photograph from which the drawing was executed.

There was nothing very difficult in making the sketches of the traps, the animals and the country. The only great trouble was to keep warm without burning my legs. It required a lot of time and patience to make drawings in the teepees. But in the end I got along and by the first of April I had a fine working knowledge of the winter life of the Indian trapper – of the manner in which he built his traps and caught the animals.

A Long Canoe Trip in Summer

This was all well enough for the mid-winter existence but it gave me nothing of the Indians' summer camps and their canoe life. So some years later, in the spring and summer of 1911, I started north from Jackfish on the north coast of Lake Superior and canoed by the Hudson Bay Long Lake Post route down the Kenogami to the James Bay country. This long canoe trip gave me a fine idea of the summer life of the Indians. I saw the coming of the fur brigades to the Post, the trading of the winter's harvest of skins, and the spending of the credit. I watched the building of the bark canoes and enjoyed the summer teepee life of the care-free trapper.

This rounded out a year's toil and pleasure of the Indian and provided as fine a working idea of them as any artist ever had or will have, for the life that I saw is fast changing.

The Ojibways, and Crees of the James Bay country were some-what different from the Montagnais of Eastern Canada. They rather liked my going about among them and they took very kindly to my sketching. They finally adopted me into the tribe and gave me the name of *Miss-a-nog-a-neegan* – "the picture-making man". And by that name I am known to this day among the Ojibway Indians of the James Bay district.

The Snow Baby

Somewhere in far north Canada lives the Snow Baby. In the Summer when the south winds wave the long pointed tops of the spruce; when the wild rice grows in the marsh and the trout lies deep in the pools, then the Snow Baby lives with the ferns and the leaves and the carpet of moss.

But when the great white blanket of Winter settles upon the plain, upon the frozen river and lake and sifts through the somber forests, then the Snow Baby is hurried by his mother into the tent-home the Indian father has made of pieces of birch-bark, laid about a frame of poles. Here, upon a carpet of fresh balsam boughs, the little brown babe crawls about in comfort, for a wood fire is burning and it is snug and warm within the teepee. Just outside this thin protection of bark, a still killing cold of fifty or more below compels not only the trappers of the North to seek shelter but the animals they hunt as well. Underneath old windfalls, under the snow itself they burrow, for strange as it may seem, the snow is a warm blanket and often protects life. But among all the furry animals that hide beneath this blanket of nature, there is one (in name at least) that lives within the man-made shelter.

So, when the thin cold yellow of the Winter sun has faded and the purple of the coming night creeps over the frozen land, when the birch trees crack from the bitter cold, then it is that you are glad to be with the Snow Baby and his mother safe within the shelter of thin bark.

With the coming of the night, a single candle is lighted. It throws great hunched shadows on the yellow bark walls of the home. From out these shadows peer the bead-like eyes of the Indian trapper as he watches the mother prepare the Snow Baby for the long sub-arctic night. The little hunter is wrapped about and about in a big furry blanket, made from more than a hundred skins of the white rabbit – the snow-shoe rabbit of North Canada. She draws upon each foot little lynx-skin socks with fur inside and pulls well down over his head a cap of fur. And when the furry bundle is put into a cradle made of a single blanket thrown across two ropes that are tied to stakes – it is then you love him best, for the little bead-like eyes are the two dark spots in all that soft mass of white and they

First published in *Little Verses and Big Names* (New York: George H. Doran Co., 1915).

Mother and Papoose; 1912.
Ink and watercolor; 14 x 17½.

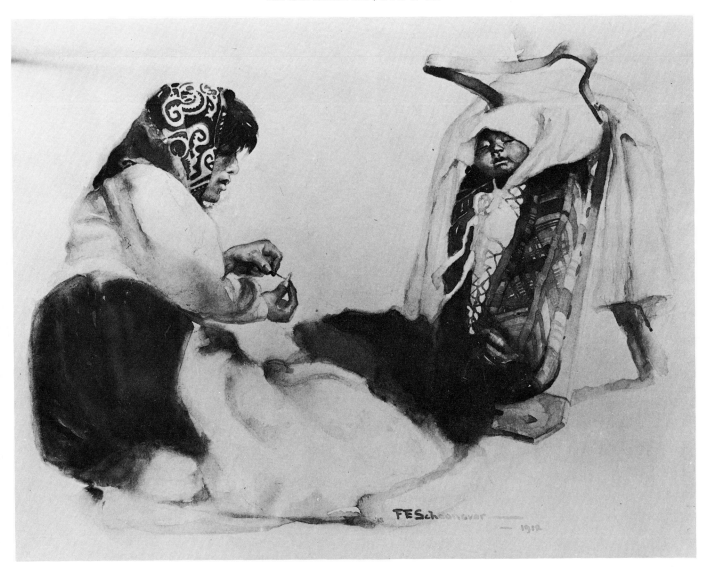

watch you, wondering what sort of a stranger you are – this reader, who has wandered into their outlandish world of stillness and whiteness.

But now the Indian mother swings the Snow Baby back and forth, singing the while a song that has been sung in just this same way, in the North, for hundreds of years. And the mighty hunter – the setter of traps for the big bear – looks on and watches and smokes and you hear him say with the trace of a proud smile:

"*Le gros uapoosh! Le gros uapoosh!*"

Which means, "The big white rabbit!"

Yes, the big white rabbit that some day will go with him along the frozen trail and help him set the traps.

And that is why, when the bitter Winter cold settles over the northland and when the animals seek shelter and do not move about – that is why some "big white rabbits" live in the man-made shelters of far North Canada.

Part Four

The
Canadian
Illustrations

Warrior's Quest; 1921.
Oil; 27 x 38.

The Barter; 1905.
Oil; 28 x 36.

Ojibwa Indian Spearing the Maskenozha (pike); 1911.
Oil; 30 x 32.

The Northwest Mountie; 1923.
Oil; 30 x 36.

Indian Sun Priest; 1927.
Oil; 30 x 34.

White Fang and Gray Beaver in Canoe; 1906.
Oil; 18 x 30.

On Leaped the Canoe like a Runaway Horse; 1924.
Oil; 32 x 48.

Descending the Mountain; 1927.
Oil; 18 x 36.

Junction of the Yukon and the Porcupine Rivers; 1906.
Oil; 16 x 24.

Wa-Gush; 1906.
Oil; 30 x 48.

Indians in a Canoe; 1916.
Oil; 40 x 34.

Mountie and Indian; 1930.
Oil; 28 x 36.

The Freezing Man Was Dragged to Safety; 1914.
Oil; 32 x 40.

The Canoeists; 1911.
Oil; 28 x 46.

Trappers on Lake; 1932.
Oil; 28 x 36.

Sinking through the Ice; 1931.
Oil; 26 x 38.

Toboggan with Body; 1919.
Oil; 30 x 36.

The Factor; 1905.
Oil; 30 x 36.

List of Illustrations